Andreas Schöler

Flirting With Life

*Travelling the world in search of freedom
and belonging*

Translated by Jack Corrigall

I

About the book

Why do we travel? What are we searching for? What do we find?

Who or what do we reach at the end of the road in the savannah? What happens after we've found our dream job and our true love in paradise?

After researching the origins of life at particle accelerators, curiosity and a hunger for life drove Andreas Schöler to travel the world for many years. He combines tales of fascinating experiences in settings as diverse as ascetic meditation retreats, lonely lakes in the Rockies and crowded mud huts in West Africa with reflections on finding meaning and happiness in life. From founding a school for salsa in the Caribbean to picking fruit in Australia, he was on a constant search for the good life and what connects us as human beings.

About the author

Andreas Schöler was born in 1978 and grew up as part of a large family in rural Germany. He studied Quantum Physics and now lives near Heidelberg with his wife and daughter. His travels have taken him to over 60 countries and he has worked on four continents. He is currently responsible for strategic global alliances in the IT sector.

*"Everything one views with love is beautiful. The more one loves
the world, the more beautiful one will find it."*
Christian Morgenstern

Contents

VIII

I would stay and love you, but I have to go

Introduction

Waves slammed against the bow of the ship and huge freighters towered out of the water like metal islands. The sea of densely packed skyscrapers on the horizon became ever clearer. An inhospitable scene. Rain thrashed against my face. The atmosphere suited my slightly melancholic mood. It was time to go again. This time it was Hong Kong that I was leaving.

In just a few hours I would be at a hedonistic party, surrounded by a display of toned, tanned bodies, some clothed in nothing more than a little body paint, the air around me impregnated with hormones, alcohol, desire and thumping beats. Bondi Beach, Sydney. My new base for the coming months. Hong Kong would quickly feel miles away, like a former life.

The pace of such a trip can be brutal, relentless. But every farewell is a new beginning: a new country, new friends and new acquaintances, different food, different jobs and a different climate. It's about finding a balance between staying and going. Between staying with people and places held dear and the promise of leaving, the magic of the new. Between freedom and belonging.

Lisa St. Aubin de Terán attempted to put this fleetingness of being while travelling, this intimate but at the same time transient dance, into words as "flirting with life":

> Travelling is like flirting with life. It's like saying, "I would stay and love you, but I have to go; this is my station."[1]

Glow worms, yogis and freedom

Prologue

I'm out of here. I'm gone. So long, suckers.

I'm off to see the world. And to find a dream job in paradise.

I'm off to rise under rustling palm trees on a white sand beach. To wake with the lingering satisfaction of a magical, Milky Way-canvassed, glow worm-lit tropical night spent in the caress of the luminescent sea, in waters with stories to tell and dreams to spark into life.

I'm off to live in a hippy community in the Australian Outback, to live in tepees, tree houses and house boats, to work hard on farms and party harder through long nights, to drift in a world in which time, in which life seems so completely different.

I'm off to discover and discuss extraordinary ways of life with yogis in New Zealand, with the authors of the New China in the futuristic metropolises of Shanghai and with extreme sport junkies in sunny California. I'm off to meet ladder-climbing lawyers in Hong Kong, nouveau-riche Sikhs in the hectic sensory overload that is Mumbai and models from New York under a canopy of Saharan stars.

I'm off to party, to celebrate life. It doesn't matter where: it can be a chic Sydney bar, an underground Shanghai club, an intercultural wedding in Berlin, a Couchsurfing meeting in Panama's Old Town or a Ghanaian chief's hut with a few kola nuts and a couple of dried fish for his wives.

I'm off to immerse myself in new worlds, to shrink the horizon in my rear-view mirror, to join turtles on a swim through the teeming colours of coral forests, to experience my own life in unimaginable oneness on a ten-day Buddhist meditation retreat.

I'm off to be free. I'm off to be here today and gone tomorrow, to look out at Sydney Harbour Bridge while turning on the air conditioning one day and toy with the idea of taking a job as a social worker on an aboriginal reserve the next. I'm off to do my head in trying to solve logistical processes while registering refugees in Johannesburg and to spend my birthday bathing in a remote glacial lake in the wilderness of the Rockies.

To travel and be free. To set off into the world as an apprentice craftsman on his journey, a young Aborigine on his outback walkabout or a romantic ne'er-do-well on his peregrinations. Or to turn my back on the familiarity of my home and set off into the great wide open with nothing more than a violin on my back and a heart full of the joys for life one beautiful midsummer's morning.[2] Travelling is liberating and inspiring. It enriches, exhilarates and educates.

Travelling is also taking leave. Transience to the power of ten. Travelling is also never settling in, perpetually moving on. Freedom is also not belonging. The path leads the journeyman, the young aborigine and the ne'er do well away from home, but it also brings them back. Wanderlust and homesickness often lie hand in hand. They can even merge into one another.

And so this book also travels between freedom and belonging, between setting out and settling in. Between recollections and reflections. It is faithfully accompanied by the search for the good life and for the little—and larger—joys in life.

Travel as a primal experience

Ghana

I'm just off to save the world
Beginnings

It all began with six months of service abroad in the field of HIV/AIDS in Ghana. It probably began before that. It was the quest, born out of my youthful idealism, to find the greatest possible challenge—something to which I could devote my life and create meaning.

There was no challenge too big and so I began with what were for me the most fundamental questions: What is time? What is space? What is matter? Why does life exist? Why does humankind exist? Why does love, language and consciousness exist? What is understanding? What is knowledge?

I studied physics because I wanted to find the answers and push the envelope of knowledge. I wanted to build on this to step into the unknown and make new discoveries. I wanted to be the first to recognise patterns, structures and relationships, and, in doing so, enter spheres bigger, grander, nobler, more infinite than our limited human existence, the boundaries of our sensory perception and the world that surrounds us.

My thirst to find explanations was as strong as my fascination for foreign cultures was later to become. I wanted to fathom what light is and marvelled at the elegance of Maxwellian equations, at how in just a few symbols they manage to explain the self-induced movement of electromagnetic waves in a vacuum. I wanted to discover the limits of determinism and human macroscopic models of explanation in quantum mechanics. I was impressed by how social dynamics and behavioural strategies can be simulated using game theory. I asked myself how the brain synchronises information and what evolutionary advantages this confidence in and awareness of ourselves as individuals and our existence as human beings has brought with it. I wanted to find out where space remains for free will and the divine in concepts such as entropy, emergence and the calculation of symmetry from fundamental interaction.

As enthusiastic as I was at first, as impressive and hugely influential the application of scientific knowledge in the form of technical "achievements" is for the modern world, they were essentially just human models and provided no answers as to why. Although the whole thing was impressive in its abstractness, in the scale of its intellectual complexity and efficiency, I increasingly questioned every intrinsic end-in-itself and felt that precisely this abstraction was increasingly distant from the priorities of my own life.

I felt more and more that reducing things to an intellectual level was a dramatic limitation of what constituted human life and humankind, of what made me. Everything that encompassed and characterised the miracle of life (or what humans can experience thereof), everything I admired in other people, everything that made me laugh and cry was so much more than the world of fundamental formulas, which failed to predict even the tiniest of "real" systems.

After the big questions of the universe came the topic of saving the world. This was a pretty obvious progression: I was the child of parents who espoused the ideals of the 1968 revolutions, dragged me along to peace marches as a toddler, shopped at fair trade shops and had a merry band of children selling waffles for UNICEF at the Christmas market.

After my first voluntary service and an eco-workcamp abroad, I naturally wanted the most global-galactic option and so it didn't take long for me to decide on six months of voluntary service in the field of HIV/AIDS in Ghana.

The organisation with which I travelled to the sub-Sahara was the American Field Service (AFS). Originally called the American Ambulance Field Service, it was, like the Red Cross, founded to help the wounded and POWs in times of war. Shortly after the Second World War, the AFS began organising various voluntary service programmes and student exchanges with the aim of preventing war through understanding between peoples.

In Ghana, I was to catch both malaria and the travel bug.

A hunger for life
Welcome to Africa

The thick, heavy tropical air surged against me. A flood of new smells and sounds poured down upon me. I was assaulted by the hectic hurry—a clamour of voices and hands grabbing at my luggage. "Akwaaba"— welcome to Ghana.

I myself, however, was wide awake. I was already in travel mode. I'd become my travel self. I was feeling lively, adventurous — a dry sponge ready to absorb the water of these new impressions. The turmoil of recent days and weeks, the doubts, the paralysing waiting around, had vanished.

One of the wonders, part of the magic, of travelling is that although preparing to leave was tough and I was reluctant to leave my loved ones, it all changed when I turned my back on my home and the journey properly began. In this moment, I was suddenly accompanied by entirely different travel companions: curiosity, a sense of adventure, a hunger for life and for the unknown.

As we flew over the Sahara, the stories of caravans, the Silk Road and the Orient miraculously awoke in an entirely new reality. Stories and history literally became something I could touch and experience. Time became a seemingly resolvable illusion.

The picture with which I was presented upon arriving in Accra was therefore all the more surprising. At the house, the other volunteers had been receiving crash courses in the language and information on the country's dos and don'ts from young Ghanaians for several days. Lethargy and frustration. Essentially the first culture shock. All these volunteers had left their homes in the Western world to see the real Africa, to be alone among black people and save the world. Instead, we now found ourselves in an industrial juggernaut. It was somehow almost entirely devoid of organisation. It was unclear as to how and when each of us was to get to our respective project. It was unclear as to how and when we were to hold a workshop (nobody really wanted to do this anyway; we wanted things to finally get real). It was even unclear as to how and when we should move out of the house to at least see a little more of Accra. What really grieved me was all these other palefaces: it didn't look like Africa one bit and all we'd done was to have spent several days stuck together in a confined space.

Another of my first impressions is still very vivid in my mind: it was when I first observed one of Ghana's smallest inhabitants. Barely audible in its smooth flight, it was slimmer than the versions with which I was familiar: the first of the mosquitoes to accompany my first shower was somehow perplexing, seemingly innocent and harmless. How could such a delicate creature be capable of transmitting so much suffering? I was to find out for myself very soon.

Although I personally found the colourful bunch of notorious "do-gooders", dreadlocked hippies and the obligatory much sought-after beauty queen quite interesting, I was also relieved when we were all gradually placed in full-to-bursting trotros or coaches and shipped off to our various projects.

Trotros are the ubiquitous minibuses of sub-Saharan Africa. Most have been completely gutted and fitted with wooden benches so that the maximum number of passengers can be squeezed in. A single row in one of these slim Japanese vans typically seats four people and this is often only possible because half of them are forced to lean forward. Essentially you are completely packed in and cannot move. In some cases you have chickens on your legs and someone's child on your lap. The question of who is getting out when is usually clarified before you get in, because it might otherwise be necessary to reload the entire bus. Another characteristic of these buses is that they only set off once they're full. In extreme cases this can take several hours. It is remarkable considering all of this that these bus journeys are an absolute highlight for many travellers in Africa. At first I also found this complete immersion, this being at the mercy of others, this skin-to-skin contact, extraordinarily exciting.

I had finally been plunged into and submerged in Africa.

The children called out "Oburoni" to me and wanted to touch my hair as they found it so exotically light and above all smooth. A fellow passenger shared sweet local mini bananas and fresh peanuts with me. I had my first experience of drinking water from small plastic bags, first biting a hole and then spitting the remains out of the window.

"Oburoni" is the local term for all white people and literally means "those who come from over the horizon". Ghanaians, in contrast, are "Obibinis"—black people. Later I was to learn how painful it can be, how alone and persecuted you can feel when you hear "Oburoni" called after you everywhere you go and when you are always seen as the white person, often with negative connotations.

For the time being, however, it was exactly what I was looking for. I enjoyed the attention as the bus slowly tootled along the palm-fringed coast.

Colourfully painted fishing boats bobbed in the sea, the smell of fried plantains from small roadside stalls wafted in on the breeze, and very slowly my excitement gave way to deep relaxation. I dozed peacefully off with my head on the shoulder of one of my Obibini neighbours.

Black stars and cocoa
The Gold Coast

Ghana. The most famous association with the country is probably The Gold Coast: the former colony was once named after its most important raw material and commodity. Perhaps some of you still remember the former UN Secretary-General Kofi Annan. Maybe one or two of you will know that the former football player Tony Yeboah is Ghanaian and that the national team is known as the "Black Stars". But that's probably about it.

Ghana lies between the Ivory Coast and Togo on the west coast of Africa. The first fortress in Sub-Saharan Africa was built in Elmina—near the village of Takoradi, where my host family lived—back in 1482. The area was one of the most fiercely contested zones between the colonial powers, as it was from here that slaves and ivory—and later gold and cocoa—were shipped in huge quantities.

In 1957 Ghana became the first West African colony to become independent from Great Britain. Until the First World War, the eastern part of the country belonged to the German colony of Togoland. This was to have its relevance for me too, since the memories of that time had not yet left some people's minds.

Ghana is a multi-ethnic state with over 50 languages and peoples: it is inhabited by native fishing peoples such as the Ewe on the coast, the famous Ashanti in the tropical interior, and the Fulbe, who live as cattle nomads in the semi-arid north.

Today there are almost 30 million people living in Ghana. Less than 20 million were living there when I visited in 2001, which says all you need to know about population growth. The country is about as large as

Great Britain, and its shape, which is the result of the drawing-board division of Africa, resembles a sheet of A4 paper.

My African family
Takoradi

A pile of letters, composed with passion and idealism, full of dreams and boundless energy, lay on the table. Smiling, optimistic faces from all over the world looked out from the attached photos. I could make out my cover letter among them. There was a medicinal smell in the humid tropical air. A corpulent, extremely uninvolved, bored-looking woman followed the fingers of a lithe, extremely talkative, superficially friendly man as they flipped through the pages.

A brief volunteer casting session. The man was a local AFS coordinator. The woman was a potential host mother, considering whether or not to take anyone home and if so, whom. A different kind of cherry-picking. I stood in the background, perplexed and increasingly restless and tired. My original notion of a family that was looking forward to me and had prepared for me had long since faded.

A little while later she went shopping and made some of the typical short visits in the local area. Another thing it took me a little getting used to was that no-one in Ghana had been waiting for you. I was to come to this realization ever more often and it was to bear ever more beautiful fruit.

The woman, who shortly thereafter introduced herself as Mawusi, eventually returned and together with her elderly mother, her two mischievous children and two domestic helpers became my warm host family.

This was my first lesson that things are simply done differently here. But it didn't by any means mean that it was any better or worse.

I found the two helpers fascinating. Fifi was primarily responsible for sweeping, various bits of shopping and relaying various messages as well as fulfilling a role as a guard. I felt he was treated almost like an animal. He scurried around, usually bent over, and tended to be ordered about by hisses and other noises. As in many other African countries, "Fifi" simply means that he was born on a Friday. Similarly, I was usually called "Kwesi" because I first saw the light of day on a Sunday. Akuma was much more closely integrated into family life and treated as an equal. She was still more child than woman and was responsible for cooking and for the children. Lumusi, the grandmother, the head of the house and above all the helpers' mistress, later explained the selection process for Fifi and Akuma. She said she always looked for young people with no family connections and from a tribe that lived a long way away so that the helpers wouldn't be tempted to steal things or go home too often.

The most fun I had was with the two children: little Adzo and her older brother Kojo. Adzo's face was a ray of sunshine when she laughed and she already embodied pride and grace despite her youth. She liked to practise African dances with me.

"Kwesi, you need to go lower. But always keep your head up. And you have to keep your posture powerful, determined," she'd say. She liked to tease me when I failed to maintain my body tension.

Kojo's big, curious eyes and serious brow contrasted with his playful nature. I often joined him on strolls along the beach or visits to internet cafés. Sometimes we exchanged stories about our so different lives.

"How can you live in a country where it is colder than a fridge?" he asked incredulously. He taught me the complex choreography of hand and finger movements with which men greet their friends in Ghana, ending in a flick of their buddy's hand.

I was also sitting with the two of them as we stared in disbelief at a small, flickering black-and-white TV on 11 September 2001. We had only the remotest of ideas of what was going on.

Ghana was another world for me and so the images from New York seemed all the more otherworldly and surreal.

Job-hopping in Africa
Looking for work

I wanted to save the world while I was in Ghana. At least a little. And experience a few things. I wanted change. I wanted to return as a new person. I wanted to make a difference.

But the pace of life in Ghana at first seemed to me to be rather lethargic, deliberating, an exercise in perseverance. Day upon day of tropical humidity, the slow trundle of the market women balancing heavy loads of papayas, pineapples, mangos and various citrus fruits or fish, manioc and yams on their heads. The long, flowery wording of the greeting ceremonies that began with a query about one's own well-being and then spiralled into an arbitrary cascade of additional enquiries about the health of one's parents, siblings, grandmothers, grandfathers, uncles, aunts, and so on.

Then there was the lunch that was prepared in the morning and then simmered for hours. This was usually a thick stew with a peanut or palm oil base into which a large, often fermented lump of dough made from manioc or rice was dropped. Eating usually took place using your hands and so the dough functioned as a kind of spoon, with which the stew was half eaten, half slurped.

Then there were the omnipresent vultures with their mighty, frayed-looking wings perched on poles, roofs and palm trees or wading through mountains of rubbish.

Even the sea sometimes seemed to swim languidly towards the shore.

Worst of all, the AFS coordinator told us on a daily basis that we would be heading off to the project the next day, that there would soon be dance and drum classes, that there would soon be a visit from other AFS volunteers. I often waited for hours until he showed up at all (wearing his usual broad grin, of course). Whenever we did manage to set out or drive off, he would stop every five steps or minutes for seemingly trivial banter and handshakes with all sorts of people. Or we'd head out to a project and end up shopping around for spare car parts. That was all normal there. The only ones who expected anything else were the other two volunteers and me.

Finally, the day came when I first entered the offices of the Planned Parenthood Association of Ghana (PPAG), the project for which I had prepared so diligently and which had been one of the main reasons I had chosen Ghana. After I had waited a few hours, my contact told me that I should come again the next day, as no activities were taking place on that day. This was repeated a few times, until I was finally told that there were no funds for the moment. In the end, I made precisely one trip with the team. We visited a remote village where the staff provided education on family planning and sexually transmitted diseases and I played the role of the town crier insofar as I, as a white person, brought the whole village together as an attraction.

Later someone made the brilliant suggestion that I visit the PPAG clinic, where, as a young Western European, I was supposed to advise couples who communicated in Fante and spoke almost no English on the topics of condoms for women and their love lives. Unsurprisingly, this idea proved to be infeasible at the very first attempt.

So what did I to do when I felt so inhibited in my need for a productive vocation and an eventful stay?

I got going. With the courage of desperation, I decided to simply go directly to various regional authorities and ministries in the field of health and education. After many attempts (the same story of empty offices, being referred at some point to someone else, etc.) a number of meetings and events came about. The bottom line, however, was usually that there was a certain presumption of benefit for the respective interest group or decision-maker: namely that contact with me might in one form or another lead to an inflow of funds.

My proactive approach did in fact end in various proposals to international development cooperation institutions, in which I attempted to summarise and prepare ideas and concepts for such things as an AIDS education programme for a youth football league and send them to the suitable persons. While this was certainly good in terms of feeling like I was finally doing something, I remained entirely unaware of any success I may have had. However, my contact at the Ministry of Education was to be of use to me in an entirely different way.

It is telling that I obtained my main job in Ghana through one of the many spontaneous conversations that began because of the colour of my skin and texture of my hair. On this occasion the conversation took place with some children on a bus. I was—as I so often am—enthused by the children's infectious lust for life, their cheerfulness, their broad smiles and their even wider smiling eyes, and so we got to talking about their lives and my life. My openness and naivety, as well as my constant need to talk quickly about what's on my mind, inevitably led us to the topic of work. And so I discovered that these kids had a science teacher who had just left his job at the school, and they liked the idea that I might take over his role.

A few days later I was standing in front of one of my three classes for the first time. Over 60 expectant juvenile eyes were staring at me and I was a little nervous. We were in the dust, in one of the typical open school buildings (a stark concrete building with simple openings for windows and doors). The children had no documents and I had a few scribbled notes on which I had compiled the lesson plan based on the curriculum I had been given: elementary physics and chemistry.

It is also typical of Ghana that within a few days I had introduced myself to the school management, received the appropriate permission through my contact at the ministry, and headed off.

At last I had a proper job.

Dancing in the dust
Dance initiation

It began with a simple rhythm banged out on the edge of a large bass drum with a stick. After a while came a busier beat played with an open palm on a smaller drum. Whip-like djembé slaps then interrupted the rhythm and a new beat developed. After a handful of drums had joined in a uniform rhythm, the first vocalists began to sing and weave their voices into the soundscape.

By this time my heart was in my mouth and my excitement had reached fever pitch. The drums had captured me as they had all the other musicians, singers and dancers. The collective excitation caused the heat shimmer in the air to vibrate at an even higher frequency. Sweat ran out of every pore of my body and dripped onto the dust below my feet.

Suddenly it was still. More beats on the djembé. After a short, tension-charged pause, a new rhythmic wave surged across the space. The arms of the drummers flew over the drumskins at an even faster, more frenetic pace. The dance began.

We jumped forward in a long line, full of explosive energy and yet in strict choreography, alternating quickly between stretching upwards with our hands held high and dropping down into a hunch with our hands on the ground.

After one round of the space, the beat changed and the men separated from the women to organize themselves in separate formation. The female dancers whirled in front of us, as if in a trance. Then it was our turn to step forward and perform our solo in combative movements. Meanwhile, the audience had joined in the chanting and the spectacle came to a climax as the men and women took it in turns to circle, flirt, come closer and then move away again.

Beats on the djembé again. We turned and rejoined the women in a line. The vehemence of the rhythms slowly subsided and after another round of less demonstrative movements, we left the space.

As a physicist and cellist who grew up in the country, it is clear that I did not exactly qualify for the Champions League in terms of coolness and the party scene.

My clubbing experience was limited to occasional trips to techno discos in the Frankfurt area.

The shock I experienced when I first went on international language courses and came into contact with young people (often from foreign metropolises) was considerable.

Anyone can drink, and my school friends and I were in no way inferior to someone from Berlin or New York in this respect. But when the dancing reached its climax during the night, I was usually one of the first to hide (in the literal sense of the word), so as not to be dragged onto the dance floor in exuberant fashion by one of the much-adored beauties.

My low point came at a disco I visited while on a language trip to England. Having done my best to overcome my fears, I ventured into the dance-floor spotlight. In order not to draw too much attention to myself, I started to dance using almost nothing but slight hand movements close to my body. That was all it took to very much amuse two pretty girls, and I wasn't seen on the dance floor again for some time.

It was time for a change.

One of the secondary reasons I volunteered in Ghana was that it is a country famous for its traditional dances and drumming. If I were to learn these very expressive, body-driven dances, I would surely conquer every dance floor thereafter. At least that was my plan.

So, after the obligatory waiting for nothing to happen with regard to the dance and drum classes the coordinator had promised, I went looking for a dancer or one of the cultural groups that put on dance performances. As a dance school is not something that would come into anyone's mind in many dance-loving countries (at least not for local dances), this was how I hoped to find a dance master.

Black and blue hands, blistered feet—I'd struck gold. Once my eagerness had led me to find not only a group that gladly welcomed me, but also a "master" who accompanied me to the practice area whenever I passed by his modest accommodation, I let loose with real determination. I then quickly felt the effect of the dusty floor and the leather drums on my white, "academic" hands and feet.

I actually gave up drumming after a short time, because my hands could barely recover and kept on swelling and bruising very quickly. Learning drumming was going to take more time than I had.

But I continued with the dancing. Although my physical abilities were a limiting factor here too (especially when I was weakened by illness on several occasions), one of the key experiences of my time in Ghana was dancing as if unleashed in the dust and tropical heat, performing warlike scenes with swords and the playful convergence of man and woman in front of numerous smiling, benevolent black faces.

Sick and alone
Malaria

It began in the night.

Diarrhoea, fever. More diarrhoea, higher fever.

And so in the morning I dragged my already feeble body to the private clinic that Lumusi had mentioned as the number one medical address in town.

And what did the number one address look like? An open concrete edifice with no windows and a long queue of people waiting on the loamy earth in front of the door in the subtropical heat.

Despite the heat I was cold and slightly light-headed as I vegetated in the scorching sun.

The diagnosis seemed clear by the time I eventually got to the front of the queue. Still, I was first sent to get a blood test. Sensibly, this was scheduled to take place in a laboratory on the other side of town.

So I trudged on, waited again and returned to the clinic.

I arrived completely exhausted and shivering. I had a boiling-hot fever of over 104°F. I was put on a drip and given ice packs.

My muddied mind attempted to concentrate on the drips being inserted. My job at the time dealt with AIDS and I wanted above anything else to make sure that new, sterile needles were opened for me. Although I was successful in this respect, it took the nurses many attempts to insert the drips. My arms looked like quite the battlefield by the time the fluid eventually ran into my veins.

Later that day I was lying alone. I could see more mosquitoes flying through the spaces where windows should have been and stinging me.

But the thing that surprised me more than this entire spectacle was that I was resigned to fate in a way I had never been before.

I wasn't agitated. I wasn't really worried.

I was just lonely.

The flow of travelling

Being on the go as a magnet for the moment

Looking back, I've often asked myself how my experience of certain deprivations (especially loneliness and illness) was so positive; how I sometimes simply couldn't get enough.

The constant flow of novelty and excitement makes you aware of so many completely new qualities you might have. It reveals entirely new strengths and resilience, a willingness to take risks and an ability to surrender to fate. Also, both in Ghana and on my later travels, it was only after a few months on the road that I discovered I had not reflected upon things or worked through them in the typical sense for some time. Instead, I had just absorbed them. My mind had been involved only in the immediate sensory experience and coping in the here and now.

I was enchanted, gripped and animated by the "flow of travel".

Being caught up in the flow of travel also means that the processing of experiences unfolds very gradually: despite being initially hesitant, it is inexorable and seeps into the pores of your life only over a long period of time.

While volunteering in particular, there were many, including myself, who expected to return from the new world as new people and experienced initial disappointment when nothing appeared to have changed. This is especially true when you feel that you have returned to your "old" life at exactly the same point you left it and time appears to have stood still. Since the roles to which you are accustomed and in which others continue to see you in this context have changed marginally (if at all), the whole journey at first appears almost to be an illusion, a chimera; the properly life-changing experiences seem strangely unreal.

The really interesting and transformative aspects of my journey to Ghana happened in accordance with the saying "Life is what happens to you while you're busy making other plans":[3] they did not occur as a result of the work I had ambitiously sought, nor did they occur as a result of my studying the language or even my drumming.

In my striving to organise, to use time effectively, to learn and get ahead, to have something to tell, in my strategic approach to the exotic and foreign, I was still trapped in the familiar patterns of thought and behaviour I had learnt. This often led to collisions with the new, different reality in which I found myself. The new world and its influence seeped slowly, almost imperceptibly into me during those moments of my days that were at first glance unimpressive.

Moments spent with my skin pressed closely against that of other passengers in a trotro as we waited, sweating, for the vehicle to fill. Gazing for hours at the market women as they set up their stalls, fascinated by the laughter, the singing, the vibrant life. Watching one of the acquaintances I had made on the street stomping manioc and plantains into a pulp in a large mortar. Walking with Kojo, my guest brother, in the street, his hand repeatedly looking for mine, our hands somehow swinging around each other. Accompanying friends to a church full of loud singing and dancing, with preachers who almost screamed themselves into a trance.

What Kojo was looking for, and what really annoyed me at first, was holding hands in public as a gesture of friendship. This was hard to bear for someone who grew up in a culture where a generous distance is expected and practised in public. The whole thing became even more uncomfortable when another travel companion on one of my tours through the wide landscape in the north of the country set up camp at night, choosing, of all the places in all the savannah in all the country, to lie down right next to me.

The various cultural sensibilities for physical distance and proximity are a recurrent topic and one of the most interesting topics you encounter when travelling. Although it means that the confrontation with other customs can be a bit too close for comfort in certain situations, few intercultural experiences have changed me and broadened my horizons as much.

Although I still find the apparent absence of distance in countries such as India to be somewhere between obtrusive and unpleasant, I now miss a certain closeness, an immediacy, a feeling of the other and of life without the intense physical contact on a "Caribbean level" in Western Europe.

The differences in the rhythm of life and sense of time between cultures are another favourite topic for travellers. Besides the ubiquitous waiting, what made a real impression on me on this, my first trip to a tropical country with so many barely industrialised areas, was the natural rhythm of day and night. Especially in places without electricity—rural villages and the corrugated iron shacks on the outskirts of towns—life rises with the sun and ebbs slowly away in the light of a few flickering candles, small fireplaces and the rising murmur of conversation after dusk.

Go and come
Linguistic convergence

Many African nation-states are defined by the arbitrary territorial demarcations that were drawn without any consideration of ethnic and linguistic borders (sometimes cutting right through the middle of them) during the course of imperialism.

One result of this is that Ghana is a multi-ethnic and multilingual country that has since (in wide areas at least) been guided to a certain self-identification as a nation state on the basis of various national myths and heroic tales, from the struggle for independence to the FIFA World Cup. This is helped by the fact that the lingua franca in Ghana is English and that it is surrounded by countries whose official language is French.

The reality of my travels in Ghana, however, was that the language—and with it the phrases used for greetings, the essentials for shopping, thank-yous and rudimentary small talk—changes every few miles. As many travellers can probably confirm, it is difficult to overestimate the power of just a few phrases in the local dialect. They are an expression of respect, of making an effort. I still smile to myself when I think of the warm laughter and friendly glances with which I was rewarded for such a greeting. One of the times this happened was as the women made their way to the next village market with their goods elegantly balanced on their heads, for hour after hour, mile after mile. I smile when I think of the few words I spoke to buy a pineapple and the fare collector's surprise to hear his own language coming from my mouth when I asked him to stop the minibus so that I could get out.

The more I travelled, the more I missed the entire spectrum of communicative approach and exchange with local people in countries where I lacked the language skills. One of my main goals in Ghana was to obtain at least a rudimentary knowledge of the local language in Takoradi. The same questions came up again: Where was I to start? How was I to find a teacher?

Via the AFS and the coordinator? The answer to that was clear. What about talking to people in the street? I tried this and found lovable people who were extremely willing and enthusiastic to invite me to their homes and share with me something of their language and life. However, as someone who has learned other foreign languages in a very structured way, I soon felt the lack of a systematic approach. So, at the same time I turned to local schools and finally—through my host brother's school—I was able to convince a teacher to give me private lessons. Everything and everyone in Ghana needs or takes its/their time or simply (or perhaps not so simply) has a different understanding of time. The combination of this state of affairs and the fact that my stay was very limited in terms of time meant that my knowledge of the language never extended beyond some basic grammatical structures and an extremely modest vocabulary. However, as I have already said, every single word was worth it.

The language of the Fante people, who are local to Takoradi, is logically called "Fante" and is one of the most widely spoken dialects in Ghana. I learnt it as "Mfantse", as the language is known by locals. Since this language is a dialect of Twi (in phonetics this is written [tɕʷi], which might provide an impression of its extraordinary sounds), I quickly also got to know the most important phrases of other dialects in Accra and Kumasi.

What impressed me most was the grammar, which was in my naïve and superficial impression at least very efficient and simple. It seemed to me to be even simpler than something like Esperanto, which was deliberately conceived as a simple language.

"*Me (re)ko to nam*"—"I go buy fish". The "*re*" turns the "*ko*" into the progressive form, so it becomes "I am going (to) buy fish". The most important pronouns and verbs comprise just a consonant and a vowel. Time is also expressed as a prefix. By adding "*na*" at the beginning you can turn the whole sentence into the past tense, and by simply adding "*a*" you can turn it into the present perfect. Of course, the details are more complex. Compared to many other languages that I have encountered in my life, the whole thing seems to be grammatically very efficient and is in this respect perhaps similar to Chinese and other analytical, less inflected languages.

One particular expression sticks in my mind because I love the idea behind it: "*Ko na bra*"—"go and come"—is the typical Fante phrase upon taking one's leave. Although a "goodbye" or "see you soon" might also be a pleasant farewell in the sense that it connects parting with reunion, "go and come" is particularly pointed in its simplicity and its balance between letting go and the equally strong call to return.

Baobab and nomads
Travel as a primal experience

The hot breath of the day slowly faded away, a light haze of dust and clay hung above the ground, the awe-inspiring mystical, primeval splendour of the baobab trees grew the deeper the burning sun sank. The fiery orb gradually buried itself in the loamy ground. The romping of children and the deftness of the day's final activities became increasingly vague in the twilight. A clinking of pots, female laughter and various scents—shea butter, peanut, millet and okra—wafted through the air, heralding the imminent evening meal. In the dwindling light the people's eyes seemed even more awake, more curious, even more radiant, more heart-warming.

After a long hike with my travel companion Sabir, a man from the little village of Dallung in the north of Ghana, we had returned to Singa, a small cluster of round huts in the middle of the dry savannah. We savoured stretching our tired legs out in front of us.

After arriving in the morning, we had been received by the village chief. The short conversation was complicated by the fact that Sabir had to translate the chief's words (as far as Sabir could understand the dialect) into a comprehensible form for me (as far as I was able to understand Sabir's English). And vice versa.

"He happy you here. You welcome."

Sabir smiled. The chief's wrinkled face changed to a broad grin and he nodded in affirmation. His skin looked as dry and furrowed as the loamy earth. He seemed to have been part of this place for as long as the mighty baobab tree on the square in the centre of the village.

I smiled back, bowed and presented him with a gift of some kola nuts and—for his wives—some small dried fish. Kola nuts are a typical gift in West Africa, especially for dignitaries. They are rolled around in the mouth and chewed for a considerable time, during which the stimulating effect of the caffeine they contain unfolds. The fish are a popular snack and are a rare and valuable treat because they have to be transported to the savannah from some way off. They had been in my luggage since I crossed Lake Volta on my journey from the south to the north of the country. In order to be prepared for such situations I had also made early attempts to seek out the kola nuts, which had—for me at least—proved difficult to find.

"Thank you very much", I returned submissively and tried to reinforce my words with a grateful look.

"You my guest", the chief continued, pointing to one of the round huts in the circle.

Afterwards, in accordance with custom, a short visit was scheduled to meet the council of elders, who were dozing in the shade of an old tree. It was only then that we had finally set out on a long day's walk to find the Fulani,[4] a nomadic cattle-herding people in the steppes. Every time I had seen a Fulani person on my previous brief trips to the north, I had felt like a winged time traveller from the Arabian Nights. And so I had resolved to visit the cattle nomads I found so exotic. When I had told Sabir, one of my many street acquaintances, of this a few days previously, he had offered to join me on my search.

Since the Fulani are constantly on the move and have to keep their distance from the Bantu farmers in order to avoid disputes or even skirmishes as a result of letting their animals graze on the farmers' land, we had not been entirely sure if or when we would meet them. But we had a guide who was familiar with the place: a local Muslim preacher who visited the Fulani for common prayer. After a few hours we had seen the first bulls and the robes of the shepherds. It had all felt very strange, like something out of a story book.

The men, who wore wide robes and turbans, looked almost like Tuareg tribesmen to me. But it was the women who really fascinated me: henna art, tattoos, lush ear and body jewellery. Our initial communication employed only gestures. Then, to our surprise, it emerged that in addition to their complex mother tongue of Ful, the Fulani understood some French. The shepherds proudly presented their long-horned cattle and the children were happy when I found I still had a few balloons in my backpack.

After sunset and a sumptuous meal, I lay on my mat in the mud hut in which the chief had let us stay. But I could barely sleep. Every move I made, no matter how slight, sent an impressive cloud of creatures flying through the air. I was still caught up in the day's euphoria. The events continued to dance up and down inside my head.

These trips to visit the small villages and nomadic peoples in the hinterland of northern Ghana were real highlights. It was here that I was finally able to feel like an intrepid adventurer and discoverer with a sense of destiny.

It is also the site of my favourite anecdote: having told me that the last white man had arrived a long time ago on a horse, the chief of an even more remote village went on to regale me of the suitability of the various women in his village for marriage.

I wandered through a parched landscape for hour upon hour as the sun slowly arced its way towards the horizon. I was burning with curiosity and a sense of discovery. It had begun at the very latest after I had survived malaria and several other tropical diseases. In spite or perhaps precisely because of all the adversities I had endured, I felt stronger and tougher than ever before, ready to set up camp for the night anywhere under the canopy of stars if I didn't reach a village. An exhilarating feeling of freedom spread through my entire being.

It's no wonder, then, that this feeling was one to which I became utterly addicted. Every free minute I had, I put on my backpack and headed for the end of the road—and onward—via lorry, ship or any other means of transport available.

In my youthful folly I wanted the "real deal", the full-on experience, and I was ready to accept the consequences. With giardia in my guts and other parasites on my skin, I quickly lost ten kilogrammes and had to submit to primitive methods of treatment such as cutting off skin with scissors for tissue samples.

At that time, I ate pretty much everything, wherever I was. I enjoyed it every time I washed under a starry sky with just a bucket of water, even if it had been left standing for days. I travelled on the cargo bed of a certain lorry on several occasions, only to discover a few days later that it had tipped over on one of the steep slopes, burying several people beneath it.

I rarely had a plan as to where or how I could stay overnight, but I had an unshakable faith that I would always find a place to sleep with loving, trustworthy people, and I was never disappointed. I travelled with a full pack (20 kg) and was completely at one with myself and the universe. I had everything I needed and felt ready for everything that lay ahead. The days to come might end alone and hungry, perhaps with stomach cramps and huge cockroaches for bedmates. Others might end at a roaring party, with a new acquaintance, or simply in peaceful silence, full of the day's wealth of impressions.

I like to call this the "primal experience" of travelling.

As well as being a feeling of freedom and independence, it is also the elusive experience of rediscovering yourself with each passing day; the experience that what you are, what you perceive as your own strengths and weaknesses, your needs and limits, depends so much on the context, the events that and the people who surround you. It is the sense of curiosity and pleasure in the unknown worlds within yourself at least as much as it is in the new external worlds of experience. Perhaps it is even the blurring and dissolving of these boundaries between these worlds.

And so this primal experience is, in a sense, the dance partner of the flow of travel, or the stargate to enter it. As an otherwise relentlessly reflective and contemplative human being, only experience and simply being remained. At the same time, like a punctured balloon, ego slowly lost its entire raison d'être and was absent for ever greater periods of time. It was completely incapable of filtering the constant flow of new experiences of the world and myself into the old categories.

Here perhaps lies the full significance of this experience for my life and the lives of many other travellers. On the one hand, the exhilaration of travelling and these new internal and external worlds; on the other, the clash of these experiences with the everyday self as soon as routine returns. The challenge of attempting to reconcile one with the other.

One way is to become an eternal traveller: no routine, no clashes, but also no place to call home and often increasing loneliness.

Having grown up in a very loving family environment with two brothers and two sisters, snug in the sleepy, peaceful atmosphere of a small country village in the hills of Central Germany, it was always only a question of time before I took the other way: settling down and calling somewhere home.

But that time had not yet come. Not by a long shot. For a good ten more years travelling was to be my main preoccupation and I was to regard everything else as a stopover and only ever temporary. The wide world was calling and travelling was to be my "home" for the time being.

Above the clouds with the world at my feet

On the road again

The steady humming and buzzing of a quiet long-distance flight; a dozing, sleeping crowd of people whose lives had been brought together in a confined space for a short period of time before they again made their way to different ends of the earth. Images drifted, came and went: some stayed longer, others passed as quickly as shooting stars.

I had been head-over-heels in love and had spent a few wonderfully fulfilling years in Berlin. As befits such a dynamic, experimental metropolis, I had painted the town's various districts red. Germany had also hosted a FIFA World Cup: a celebration with friends during which I had found the country of my birth to be refreshingly sunny, cosmopolitan and inviting.

What had happened to my big ideals and plans in the nearly six years since Ghana? How had Ghana manifested itself?

My search had continued. Travelling and work placements in Africa and Central America, intense part-time studies in politics and anthropology, a new city (Berlin), new languages (Spanish, Chinese), new plans.

My examination of the contemporary challenges of international politics, development cooperation and the sustainability movement led me to view renewable energies as an issue of key importance for such diverse goals as peace, rural development, sustainable growth, climate and nature protection, as well as the protection of indigenous peoples.

Although working with various NGOs and charities both in the countries where they were active and in Germany had proved to be an enriching experience and had brought me into contact with many enthusiastic, inspiring people, it had also raised many questions. As well as the fundamental purpose, motivation and long-term effects, these primarily concerned the efficiency of the measures and the personal dimension.

Is it more efficient to install solar cells on a roof in Uganda or to influence legislation in Germany to promote renewable energies in order to facilitate much wider and faster spread of these technologies via free market forces? How much can I actually achieve in an NGO, when I often only get part-time or temporary jobs and end up standing on the street canvassing for donations?

I was very fortunate to find the perfect job in the circumstances: one on the interface of politics and business. I began working in export promotions at a private (yet semi-public) renewable energies institution.

My extremely high quality of life during these years was primarily due to the new communities to which I felt a sense of belonging. There were young colleagues at my new job in lively Berlin who shared my enthusiasm for a better world through sustainable energy and with whom I hit the town after work. There was the AFS community, to which I remained closely connected through preparatory and follow-up work for further generations of volunteers as well as through organisational work (I felt in the right place both in terms of the work I did and the people I worked with at the AFS). There was also my new international circle of friends. This included many Latinos, and their lust for life, expressiveness and physical closeness attracted and inspired me.

I felt young, strong and confident. I had a degree certificate in my pocket, a good job, a fulfilling social life and the world at my feet. But despite this (or perhaps because of it), my wanderlust had become all the more powerful, all the more definite. There had to be more to life. The richness, abundance and rapture of the experiences of travelling were calling me more than ever before.

I'd already turned 29. Working holiday visas and cheap world travel tickets were only available until you turned 30. It was time to escape. Properly. Sell or give away all of my meagre processions. Check. Negotiate a sabbatical or an option of returning to my job. Not happening? So much the better. Off I went. A 40-litre backpack, a plane ticket and a 10,000 Euro budget. On the road again.

This time I had no plans for what was to come. Fantastic. From that point onward there would be no more news, no more adverts, no more television, no more Hollywood films, no more "I must, I should, I need". No preconceived dreams, ideals or goals. I was going to discover the world and who I was, what I could do, what I wanted and where I wanted to go. I was heading off to go with the flow. I was full of confidence and curiosity, full of trust in both the world and myself.

Coriander, ashrams and Ganesha

India

How people celebrate, hope and love
In travel mode

India is challenging. India is too much, an imposition. India is overwhelming, fascinating, beguiling. India is ambivalence.

It was also the first country on my route when I left Germany in 2007 with a round-the-world ticket in my pocket. I wanted a spiritual journey along the same lines as the 2010 film *Eat, Pray and Love*. I also wanted to learn about the ambitious, up-and-coming India of IT and MBAs.

The first thing I did after setting foot on Indian soil—and something I later replicated in other countries—was to purchase a local SIM card and quickly save the many contacts I had already established through NGOs and Couchsurfing. Sightseeing was not on my agenda. I wanted to get a feel for the everyday life of people in the metropolises of the various countries. I wanted to talk about dreams, worries and life goals, to cooperate, to learn, to make friends, to get an idea of the social dynamics and a sense of the meaning and expression of community and faith in the respective cultures. I wanted to experience how the joy of life is lived out in different places, how people dream and celebrate, how people hope and love.

I had sated my curiosity for volcanoes, waterfalls, temples, hostels, palaces, beaches and museums as travel goals long before I set out on this great journey. This time I wanted to plunge in and immerse myself, to lose myself and find myself again in new ways of life, to find resonance in new people and new gods.

Each of us is trying to find our way in the time we spend on our blue planet, so what could be more exciting than experiencing first-hand the different ways of life—or rather arts of living—that other human beings have developed and live? We are, after all, all brothers and sisters with an almost one hundred percent shared evolutionary history and genetics.

I was not travelling as a scientific anthropologist, and I didn't visit tribes in Papua New Guinea, the Amazon or Central Africa. My search was more modest and practical. I was looking for different ways of living in the modern, globalized world. To put it in as a business consultant would, I was searching for and experiencing best practices in order to develop a new blueprint for my own life and then fill it with life.

A cacophony of the senses
Mumbai

Khan, my Couchsurfing host in Mumbai, carefully gathered up his impressive locks and tied his turban with meditative concentration. I won't even begin to describe the time-consuming twisting of his beard.

Suitably impressed, I asked Khan how on earth he managed to do it. He bobbed his head a little. "Practice, practice, practice", he grinned.

His mother prepared us a fantastic breakfast of hearty aloo paratha (wheat flatbread filled with potatoes, plenty of fresh coriander, chillies and other aromatic spices) and mild lassi.

"Delicious!", I said as I tucked in and Khan's mother's eyes lit up.

We'd barely hit the street before I was almost knocked flat by a wave of pungent smells and deafening noise: baking heat, rotting rubbish, children relieving themselves in the roadside dust, blaring rickshaws, loud swearing, heartfelt laughter and the almost obligatory begging. It was a genuine cacophony of the senses. This was incredible India[5] in all its glory.

"See you later", said Khan, now nicely turned out in a suit, and headed off to his managerial job at a large bank in one of the new air-conditioned glass towers, somewhat removed from the madding crowd.

I made my way through the rubbish, across roadside living rooms and past several cows. As I did so, I was bowled over, enchanted and repelled by the spectacular celebration of life that surrounded me: the multitude of faces, the diligently hectic, gesticulating traders by the cluster of emaciated people sleeping on the street, the flood of stimuli embedded in wafting lethargy and crippling heat.

The intensity of activity escalated yet again as I pushed my way through the crowds at Victoria Terminus (subsequently to become known as Chhatrapati Shivaji Terminus) a little later. I wanted to take one of the infamous rush-hour commuter trains to Bendra. A sizeable amount of adrenaline pulsed through my veins as I tried to press through the thick mass of people. They couldn't have been more densely packed. This was India up close and personal. When the train got rolling, some people had been pushed out so far that a single arm was their only means of hanging on to the carriage. Others had already taken evasive action and were on the roof. Ever more passengers jumped onto the moving train, grabbing hold of anything they could—more often person than train—to stay on board. There was a certain amount of comedy to the spectacle and once we established our ponderous, jolting crawl through Mumbai's slums, tanneries and mountains of rubbish, I found myself back in the flow of travelling. I was full of wonder and enjoyed the light breeze on my face.

The throng expanded every time the train stopped and after a few stations it became clear that it was necessary to engage in near-violent pushing several stops before my desired station if I was to inch forward and gain the opportunity to disembark. My profuse apologies were met with friendly smiles. The equanimity of the Indians—in outward appearance at least—is impressive. I exited the compartment in a movement that was half jumping of my own accord, half eruption from the melee.

Wet through with sweat and with a ringing head from all the commotion, I found myself in the next chaos: hundreds of rickshaws, taxis and pedestrians swarmed in the gloaming. I didn't know the way to the bar where Khan was expecting me for our

Couchsurfing meeting so I squeezed into a rickshaw. It was, however, often unclear whether we were moving sideways or forward. The physicist in me experienced this erratic movement as a kind of Brownian motion and I smiled at the thought of how Einstein would have felt in this position.

"What happened?", laughed Khan as my exhausted frame landed in his embrace some time later. He appeared as fresh as he had done that morning. His turban and beard still looked perfect.

Idealistic adventurers and yoga
The longing for belonging

A boom in online dating sites driven by match-making parents, big billboards featuring European babies for the nouveau-riche suburbs that have sprung up in recent years, and "whiteners" (popular whitening creams for a lighter complexion) are just as much India as the meditation retreats, yoga and ashrams.

For centuries, the spiritual world of the Indian subcontinent has been a subject of fascination in the West. Various practices (yoga, reiki, meditation, etc.) are probably more popular today than ever before. In Germany, figures such as Schopenhauer and Hesse, as well as phenomena such as the back-to-nature *Lebensreform* movement of the late nineteenth and early twentieth centuries were among the many that drew on Far Eastern ideas as a source of wisdom. In one form or another, these ideas constituted what were perceived as deficits in Western culture and society, and aimed to correct them.

Just as Protestant ethics inspired capitalism, many of these techniques would appear to be a good fit for the dominant rationalist, secularist and above all individualist paradigm of the Western hemisphere. Such techniques offer irrigation for the spiritual drought of our time and are (at least as most often taught and applied) completely in line with individual, ego-focused personality development, "finding oneself" and current trends such as mindfulness and the slow movement. Yoga and the like are easy to package as weekend retreats, detox weeks or evening classes. This makes it easy to integrate them into your daily routine and to assign them a fixed time slot, just like the other things in your life.

The high demand for these techniques seems to be an expression of a longing for spiritual and mental balance, for stillness and peace, for inner strength and a sense of belonging. Although they largely allow an individual path that bypasses institutions and obligations, another important part of their attraction is that they promise to bridge the painful anonymity and atomization of "modern life" through awareness of the connectedness of all being.

As a result, spirituality has also become part of the individual's personal responsibility, something that the person in question practises on a yoga mat or meditation cushion in the confines of his or her own room. It fits the modern desire and demand to have everything under one's own responsibility and control. It is also linked to the hope or assumption that many who have found "enlightenment" through self-discovery will take greater responsibility for the social and ecological environment and, in so doing, create a better world.

But is this path of the individual's assumption of responsibility, of seeking happiness as a personal journey, really a path of salvation? Or is it a consumption-driven cul-de-sac that actually further promotes individualisation and further undermines solidarity and belonging as the basis for a shared life as part of a community?

And then there is freedom, the central value of Western culture. When is it actually liberating, exhilarating and intoxicating? And when is it solitude, loneliness, rootlessness and not belonging? Do many individual adventurers make a happy, functioning community or does lasting happiness arise only in and from community?

One of the most popular ashrams is the Osho Ashram, which was founded by Chandra Mohan Jain. The late guru was as colourful as he was controversial and his legacy (which includes writings and lectures as well as the ashram) has now become a multi-million-dollar business.[6] I slowly began to find out more about the ashram, and as my curiosity for this phenomenon grew, I decided to take a few courses there. I thought that the commercialisation and sheer size of this institution was bound to result in a wide range of options and that the large number of travellers from all over the world would at least make for some interesting exchanges.

In India, Osho achieved fame as a sex guru; in the USA he was famous for his flotilla of Rolls-Royces. Today, his fame is mainly down to the legacy of his life-affirming philosophy, which included consumption, luxury and sex. This led to conflicts with the Indian and US governments. It also meant he was opposed to the ascetic teachings of Gandhi. He has now become a pop icon in the vein of Che Guevara: the real person, his life and his achievements are irrelevant or have been completely romanticised for most of those who wear his face on a T-shirt.

The market value of the Osho brand now lies in the fusion of Far Eastern wisdom and positive psychology. This is reflected in more dynamic and less ascetic practices than typical of this cultural realm. As Osho said, "We have to change this world by celebrating, by dancing, by singing, by music, by meditation, by love, not by struggle."[7]

Whether it is a relic from another era of the ashram or whether it is a lasting expression of the fact that sexuality is also part of this celebration of life or part of spiritual union, my adventure ended at the entrance of the ashram in Pune when I was unable to present an AIDS test. And so I was to have to wait until Australia before I finally entered a meditation retreat.

The ten-dollar extra

A day in Hollywood

A large elephant stood in the magnificent entrance hall, decorated with yellow and red petals. Spread out before me outside was a lake surrounded by lush tropical vegetation. The tone in which we were addressed was somewhere between harsh and humiliating: we were, after all, mere extras on a measly 10 US dollars for a full day on a Hollywood flick filmed in Bollywood. Enough at least for a day of shoestring travelling in India. In the dressing room I had found a swanky slim-cut suit that appeared to be tailor-made for me. It had been an amusing spectacle, a metamorphosis of a different kind when the ragged band of backpackers and loose-robed Western seekers of meaning suddenly emerged from the wardrobe department suited, booted and done up to the nines. Now all we had to do was wait. The feeling was that most of us would not be involved that day. A few large pots were laid out on the street for us extras and plastic plates were pressed into our hands. Any momentary expectation of being served together with the film crew in the hotel was quickly exposed as a foolhardy illusion.

Luckily, I got the nod at some point and of course everything had to happen very quickly from then on. There were brief instructions on the desired gestures, the clapper opened, the clapper shut, and the main actor strutted gallantly in. It was in that moment that my movie career began and ended. It marked the beginning of my abstinence from Hollywood fodder. It was probably the first big cooperation between one of the booming Bollywood producers and MGM. Titled *The Other End of the Line*, it was about a pretty Indian call

55

centre agent who falls in love over the phone with a man from San Francisco. After the obligatory hurdles, the story naturally ends happily ever after.

Shacks in the monsoon
Questioning India

One of the most lasting impressions I have of India is of the many people sleeping on the street. They slept in every possible and impossible position: in baskets, on market stalls, on cars, most often directly on the asphalt, sandwiched between rubbish and faeces. Once I saw a very pretty girl wearing a colourful dress and little earrings. She looked like a princess, but instead of being in a four-poster bed, she was lying on the pavement on a street corner, next to a pile of dog dirt.

The other striking experience was the contrasts. The simple corrugated-iron shacks in front of the Hilton and the stock exchange that rose out of the slums. A visit to an event for a new luxury district while thousands of people's tarpaulin dwellings collapsed under the water of each coming monsoon. Modern buildings being constructed with bamboo scaffolding. On the one hand, callousness and phlegmatic indifference: neglected children playing alone in the dirt, relieving themselves in the street. On the other, hectic, bustling dabawalas delivering lovingly home-made food for sons, daughters and spouses to enjoy.

Another image that burnt itself into my mind are the slums right on the main roads.

A living room on the street: a few colourful depictions of Ganesha on the concrete wall. A bag of rice hanging beside them. A mother, sitting in the typical deep squat, washing her child in the gutter of a busy road. A small collection of metal pots rattling every time a lorry passes.

Some neighbouring corrugated-iron dwellings were several storeys high, but almost only if they were on a bridge, because the others were washed away as soon as the monsoon set in.

I wonder what Gandhi would say. Would he feel more comfortable in one of these living rooms or in one of the glass palaces? He'd probably be uncomfortable in both. His dream of a simple, rural India with strong local and largely egalitarian communities seems to have been shattered by the waves of capitalism. And so has his goal of an Indian subcontinent united across religious boundaries.

India as a strong force for an alternative, more social, spiritual capitalism? Or India as a follower, brutally imposed upon by capitalism; a country that assumes this economic system largely unchecked to the neglect of its own traditions in the long run?

Bollywood as a copy of Hollywood or as an expression of a uniquely Indian path?

At home all over the world

Couchsurfing

A short lived real utopia
The Couchsurfing phenomenon

Even though I had planned my trip around the world without ever having heard of Couchsurfing, it was, as a platform for hospitality and a global family, central to my journey.

Coordinated online but lived offline, this community created one of the most wonderful feelings in my life: the awareness that through Couchsurfing I had friends I hadn't met yet all over the world and that I would find a home anywhere in the world with generous, loving people who would welcome me with open arms.

The Couchsurfing phenomenon encompassed Couchsurfers in almost every country in the world and included cities such as Sydney, Mumbai, San Francisco, Paris, Berlin, Moscow, Dubai and even Shanghai.[8] Couchsurfing was life-defining for many members, as they used the site to organise a huge number of activities and of course travel. Completely new existences were established as "permanent hosts", who more or less continuously took in guests, and "permanent surfers", who stayed on couches in every country in the world.

It was nothing less than a real utopia. It was an extraordinary phenomenon that, against all reason, functioned successfully. It was a community like no other. It was place of unique trust, respect, tolerance, openness, optimism, enthusiasm, idealism, inclusiveness and love.

It was also an ephemeral phenomenon: a unique flowering of the space-time continuum, spun from the dreams and euphoria of its members rather than from reality, and more fragile than the delicate wing of a butterfly.

Couchsurfing basics
The www.couchsurfing.com platform

Couchsurfing was founded as a non-profit organisation in 2003: a time before the modern hegemony of Facebook and before Airbnb. The story behind the origin of Couchsurfing begins in the lasting impression left upon 25-year-old computer programmer Casey Fenton when he travelled to Iceland in 1999. Fenton managed to gain access to a large number of email addresses of students at Reykjavik University. He asked if he could stay with one of them and was overwhelmed by the large number of responses and invitations he received. Spoilt for choice, he eventually decided to stay with a blues musician. The hospitality and the authentic intercultural encounter proved to be an even more surprising and formative experience for him. The musician showed Fenton "his" Iceland and took him in like a good friend. Fenton wanted to make this intense, horizon-expanding experience available to others. Couchsurfing as an idea was born and a domain was registered.

Anyone was able to register on Couchsurfing and create a profile. Members were able to introduce themselves and their interests. The decisive factor was that the platform also offered question categories such as "What connects you to Couchsurfing", "What is your philosophy of life?", "What would you like to teach others?", "What would you like to learn", "What have been particularly impressive experiences in your life?". Members were also able to upload pictures.

The profile made it possible to interact with other Couchsurfers. The first way for a traveller to do this was to ask local Couchsurfers for either a "a couch" (i.e.

overnight accommodation) or "a coffee" (i.e. a meeting). Local groups quickly established themselves, organising all kinds of activities on corresponding subpages. These encompassed everything from meeting up for drinks, potluck dinners and game evenings to hikes, trips and later big Couchsurfing festivals that lasted several days.

Every interaction with other Couchsurfers could be rated by giving the other person feedback. This feedback then appeared on the other person's profile and could not be deleted. Another form of online interaction was to connect as friends and communicate via the proprietary messaging system.

Additional trust was achieved via postal verification of identity and address, with vouching being the highest label of trust. You could only vouch for someone else if you had already been vouched for three times yourself. Although at first only a small group could vouch for others, increasing numbers of members were able to obtain this status as a result of positive experiences recorded using the process described above.

That was it: the stage was set.

The virtue of hospitality
Fathoming the magic of Couchsurfing

How was it that this technological platform gave rise to such a unique community?

The search for the roots and ingredients of this very special experience of the early Couchsurfing community stretches back far into the history of humankind.

When I try to understand what value a behaviour such as hospitality has for people and their experiences, the insight into other cultures and especially the representation and evaluation of this behaviour in religions and customs is often extremely enlightening. Hospitality seems to have been a central virtue of high social value in many cultures and was often even one of the most fundamental expressions and duties of a faith.

Why? What fundamental function of hospitality could explain such an attribution of meaning?

The Greeks used the word "xenia" to describe the ritual of hospitality. This concept was based on mutual duties and, as in other cultures, went far beyond mere board and lodging to include the protection and defence of a guest. The guest in turn had particular normative duties such as respect and politeness as well as the presentation of a gift if possible. Being a good host was one of the key determinants of social standing. To receive a guest in an unsuitable manner meant a drastic loss of honour for the Greeks and other cultures.

Especially in the great monotheistic world religions, but also in cases such as that of the Greeks, importance is increased by the fact that according to the holy scriptures the guest could always be God or an angel.[9] This made hospitality nothing less than the ultimate test of practised faith and ethics. In this case, friendliness, generosity, mercy, peacefulness and love of strangers was to be expressed in the purest form as charity and love of God.

But it wasn't just religion that viewed hospitality as being of fundamental importance. The first encyclopaedia of the Enlightenment described it as "the virtue of a great soul that cares for the entire universe through the ties of humanity."[10] One of the most beautiful formulations of this in German is "*eine der liebenswürdigsten Tugenden, die je die menschliche Natur geziert hat*" ("one of the most endearing virtues to have ever graced human nature").[11]

But there are other aspects that are of key importance of hospitality with regard to culture and religion. Particularly in times when humanity consisted of the first large territorial empires and many thousands of smaller communities, in times when the distinction between friend and stranger was very stark, hospitality meant the possibility of travel. It meant the possibility of trade over greater distances and the possibility of missionary work. It also meant the possibility of building—at least temporarily—a bridge beyond faith, nationality and language, the possibility of meeting strangers in peace and as equals.

Alone the momentous nature of making international trade possible is central, since trade has always been among the most intense forms of human exchange and cooperation across the borders of individual communities. As an exchange of goods as well as technologies and ideas, trade has also always been among the most decisive fundamental driving forces of human history.

So hospitality is of importance for more than just travelling. We all have a generous, cordial host in us.

As I have already mentioned, I grew up as part of a large family in a sleepy, rural German village. The long years of my childhood and youth were the most important part of my life and took place in a small, largely isolated community that offered great closeness, trust and love. The contrast that the anonymous metropolis of Berlin posed was at first overwhelming: the seemingly unlimited possibilities, the social playground, the variety of people, the wide range of cultures and foods, the experimental subcultures, the hectic pace, the tall buildings and the many hours spent underground on the metro.

Whenever I was on a longish metro journey, one thought more than any other helped me to brighten up the depressing atmosphere of the largely grim faces surrounding me: I imagined myself as a guest of these people, with them welcoming and eager to be at their most charming: friendly, smiling, open, warm-hearted, benevolent, kind and loving.

The human family circus
Another trail

Another trail on the search for an explanation as to the phenomenon and roots of Couchsurfing leads back to the late nineteenth century.

Dark, heavy clouds on the horizon, a rising tension in the air that permeated all life. Something was brewing. An inferno on the doorstep.

Białystok. A city where Polish, Russian, Yiddish and German were spoken, and where each of these languages was also represented by a large section of the population. A city that was first under Polish, then Prussian, then Russian rule, then occupied by Germany and is now part of Poland. A melting pot.

In such a town a sensitive nature feels more acutely than elsewhere the misery caused by language division and sees at every step that the diversity of languages is the first, or at least the most influential, basis for the separation of the human family into groups of enemies. I was brought up as an idealist; I was taught that all people were brothers, while outside in the street at every step I felt that there were no people, only Russians, Poles, Germans, Jews and so on. This was always a great torment to my infant mind, although many people may smile at such an "anguish for the world" in a child. Since at that time I thought that "grown-ups" were omnipotent, so I often said to myself that when I grew up I would certainly destroy this evil.[12]

Early in my life I thought that a significant part of the tragic ambivalence of life was that many of the great ideas and achievements of humanity (whether on a personal, social or spiritual level) are conceived and born in deep crises.

The great cataclysms of the early twentieth century and their harbingers in the late nineteenth century also came at a time in which significant ideas formed by hope and love arose out of deep despair and boundless suffering.

L.L. Zamenhof, the author of the lines quoted above and an ophthalmologist of Jewish descent, developed from his childhood experiences in Białystok and later in Warsaw the vision of a human family moving closer together by dissolving linguistic separation.

On a neutral language basis,
understanding one another,
the people will make in agreement
one great family circle.[13]

To achieve this he developed Esperanto, a language that is easy to learn, uses simple grammar and which in terms of vocabulary combines a whole kaleidoscope of existing languages.

Today, numerous studies have shown that Esperanto is indeed considerably (by several factors) easier to learn (at least for a sound basic knowledge) than other languages. There are also a few million speakers of Esperanto. During Zamenhof's life there were a proliferation of global Esperanto movements with local groups and even world congresses, which culminated in the narrowly rejected initiative to establish Esperanto as the language of the League of Nations, the predecessor of the UN.

Another of Zamenhof's projects was even more ambitious. In an attempt to bridge the gaps between people presented by race, culture, nation, language and faith, he developed his own philosophy of life. His ideal was people who are aware of their attachment to humanity and a common ethic as opposed to people who separate themselves as strangers and enemies using nationality, language and religion. This philosophy was known as "homaranismo" and was based on a version of the golden rule that appealed to the common core of all credos: "One should treat others as one would like others to treat oneself."

The intimacy and vulnerability of receiving someone as a guest as well as being at the mercy of someone else as a guest are situations in which one can best learn, practice and experience this rule.

Esperanto and Zamenhof were a decisive influence on Servas, the first global hospitality network and most important predecessor of Couchsurfing. And even if English is now the neutral language for the basis of understanding, Zamenhof's goal of connection between people through their humanity and his philosophy of life constitute the core of that which makes the Couchsurfing community special.

Peacebuilder
The spirit of Couchsurfing

Looking back fifty years from now, my heart overflows with joy as I remember the kindnesses, the thoughtfulness, patience and generosity I encountered almost daily as a questing vagabond. Call it a pilgrimage into the soul of humanity, if you like. My temple was the world; my fellow parishioners the human family; my bible the sermons of the lives of the people in all social strata.[14]

In Esperanto, the word "servas" means "we serve", in the sense of "we serve peace". This was the name given to hospitality network originally christened "Peacebuilder" by its founder, Bob Luitweiler.

Luitweiler was born in Bellingham, in the northwest of the USA, near the Canadian border, in the year that the Second World War ended. This idyllic city lies on the water in a kind of fjord with a panoramic backdrop of mountains that rise up to around 10,000 feet. Today it is a showcase city for renewable energy and has been commended for its high quality of life.

In 1907, it was the scene of the Bellingham Riots, in which a white mob beat Indian workers, looted their homes and drove them out of the city.

Luitweiler grew up under the strong influence of Gandhi's non-violence movement and refused military service during the Second World War, an act for which he was imprisoned. He used his time there to learn Esperanto and to deal more intensively with questions of peace, society and community. The limitations of the knowledge gained by social movements and societies through academic study were obvious to him early on, and so, after regaining his freedom, he began travelling in search of a path towards a world of greater peace and solidarity.

Above all, I wanted to know those movements that had been most successful in awakening a strong sense of social consciousness among ordinary folk. I was looking for credible foundations for a nonaggressive democratic society. Experience and study of social movements had convinced me that this was the best route to developing a more just social system.[15]

This search immediately led him to the Danish Folk High Schools. Luitweiler considered appropriate education (particularly the education of young people and young adults, and above all education for "ordinary" people) as perhaps the most effective way to achieve a better society and so found the idea of a School for Life[16] very promising and attractive. This concept has its origins in the thinking of the Danish pastor N.F.S. Grundtvig. The school has no grades or certificates and is based on community and practical learning, social responsibility, meaning and spirituality. Brief aside: this idea influenced world history. A US school built on this model became the cradle of the social rights movement: it was where Rosa Banks, Martin Luther King, Jr. and others studied.[17]

Luitweiler travelled to post-war Germany in order to understand how something like the world wars could happen and how to effectively prevent a recurrence. He searched in the new nation state of Israel to gain experience of community life on kibbutzes. He went to India to learn about the non-violence movement and the rural development programme that Gandhi had initiated. He wanted to understand, but what he really wanted was an exchange with people. He looked everywhere for the seeds for a better world.

All over the world there are small groups and individuals who are working for a society based on creative vocation, non-violence and social responsibility.[18]

He found such groups everywhere. Even in devastated Germany, he discovered the anthroposophy movement, the educational institutions of the trade unions and self-sufficient local communities.

Everywhere he went, he planted the seed of his own idea, Peacebuilder. He tried to find hosts and set up local committees. Under the motto "Open Doors for Peace and Friendship" he attempted to give people the chance to broaden their horizons, see connections and learn from and with people from other societies so that they would become ambassadors and catalysts for peace.

One of the dreams of those who started Servas was to help open-minded people experience these oases of sanity and generosity in a splintering, a disillusioned world and then apply some of what they had learned when they returned home.[19]

Today Servas is a global NGO and is recognised by the UNO. It serves international understanding and is somewhere between a voluntary service and Couchsurfing. Since other organisations used the new opportunities for communication offered by the internet earlier and more intensively, the number of exchanges using Servas is now relatively low. There was, however, a positive aspect to the barriers presented by sending cover letters and receiving letters of invitation by post, cumbersome contact with local organisations and potential hosts when I set off on my trip: it was as a result of this that I decided to go with Couchsurfing.

But the spirit of Zamenhof and Luitweiler, of Esperanto and Servas, lives on in every one of the other hospitality networks. And every single exchange, no matter how short, is both a giant leap for mankind and almost certainly a wonderful, formative experience for both guest and host.[20]

Frozen lava and beaming eyes

Love on the road and Couchsurfing dates

On the evening before my thirtieth birthday I emerged from my tent a little chilly, limbs pleasantly tired from the long hike. I felt alone and at the same time in a state of blissful calm. On the other side of the lake I saw the mighty ice of the glacier rolling powerfully, majestically down the mountain like a frozen lava trail. Complete silence. The still glacial waters stretched out before me. I marvelled at the sharp-edged stars and the almost full moon, reflected on the lake as golden lanterns flickering between the imposing mountain flanks.

The next day, having been woken early by the cold, I quickly slipped into the nascent morning's flood of summer light. I was so taken by this natural spectacle that I stopped, spellbound for a while. As the sun slowly climbed the mountains, its rays fathomed ever-new contours in the ever-warming light. They rolled across imposing ridges, setting the green of the trees alight and paintbrushing the boards of the little rowing boat a little way in front of me before caressing my face.

Later, I took a dip in the lake. The overwhelming beauty, my deep sense of humility in the face of creation and my gratitude at being part of this whole led me to experience it as a near-sacred act of cleansing.

When, with beaming eyes, I told Luba about this stirring moment a few days later, I'd moved on again and was thousands of miles from this glacier in the mountains of Canada's west coast. I'd met Luba at a Meetup event[21] just a few hours before. Now we too were sitting under an amazing canopy of stars.

Perhaps it was even reflected in her joyful eyes. Who knows?

Shortly after arriving in New York, I had set off for Acadia National Park with my Couchsurfing host and others from the Meetup group. Despite having travelled through the entire night, the fresh air and beautiful scenery awoke an unrestrained childish urge to charge off into nature. After a day of hiking and mountainbiking, we saw out this mini-lifetime looking out from an idyllic hill.

Luba sat next to me by one of the national park's many lakes and stared out at the expanse of water before us. She spoke quietly—half to herself, half to me—so as not to disturb the silence around us.

"What a wonderful moment. Can you see how many stars there are here and how clear the Milky Way is? Isn't it crazy that we were in the concrete jungle of Manhattan just yesterday?"

She turned and looked me in the eyes. "How is it for you? Don't you get tired of so many magical moments after a certain amount of travelling? Don't they lose their intensity? Don't they become blurred and interchangeable?"

I took a moment to gather my thoughts. Partly because I had to think about it and partly because her direct gaze seemed to pierce me in a pleasant, curious, gentle manner. How was it possible? We had only known each other for a few hours and yet I felt so close to her. Her voice and eyes seemed so familiar. I'd very probably shared more important thoughts and dreams with her that day than with many other older friends. The radiance of the day and the forests and lakes that surrounded us sparked thoughts into life and we let our imaginations run wild. We knew that we only had that day and the day after. As often on my travels, it was clear from the outset that we would only have a few hours in which to find out everything we wanted to know about the other person. Just a few hours together to experience everything we wanted to share. Transience magnified, a relationship in time lapse.

"There are definitely experiences that lose their appeal or novelty on this kind of trip. Some actually get stressful or tiring. I've even got to the point where I've felt sick of travelling or a little bit overwhelmed by the new stimuli and events. But that's mainly to do with things like the whole logistics of travelling or the constant moving on, even if you want to stay."

I turned my eyes to the night sky.

"Really magical moments are rare and precious moments, even when travelling, and like most things in life, you can never plan them. The only times that a starry sky touched me in a similar way on this trip were at the glacial lake in Canada and near Uluru in Central Australia. I was lying on a camping bed with the imposing Southern Cross above me and the earthy red of the Outback in the light of the night sky. I was still high on the mysticism and energy of the hike around Uluru and somehow the form of the Southern Cross made me aware of the transient nature of life, of my life. How many more times would I see this cross in my lifetime? How often would my life take me so far abroad?"

I still felt Luba looking at me and caught her eye. I didn't fight the feeling that her eyes were slowly filling my entire body. We came closer together and enjoyed each other's presence while we continued to talk. It was only natural that at some point we were lying in each other's arms, lips touching.

We wanted to stop time and stay in this embrace in this place at this moment forever.

Some Couchsurfers treat the website as a kind of dating platform and many more non-Couchsurfers probably regard it as such.

Is it? How does that fit with everything I've said about hospitality and understanding between peoples?

First of all, most of us are familiar with the Spring Break or summer holiday effect: the combination of a great time, lots of sun, air and sea, lots of partying, dancing, letting loose and having fun. And if you share this with good people, it's no surprise that it sometimes leads to flirting or discovering your true love.

If you've ever backpacked through South-east Asia with a Lonely Planet guide, gone Interrailing in Europe or done the Coast to Coast in South Africa you'll know that in traveller communities of intrepid, unattached young people who have set out to experience life in all its fullness, connections and experiences between people are a normal, beautiful and important part of the adventure—as they always are in life. The foreign element and the often long periods of being alone serve to magnify the sense of unity.

For solo travellers in remote and difficult regions, and for Couchsurfers who actually surf and host in other countries there is another essential element: Who goes on such a trip? Who has the courage, the resources, the audacity, the self-confidence, the trust, the curiosity?

When used as an approach to travelling in strange, sometimes remote regions, Couchsurfing requires a great deal of tolerance, trust, respect, do-gooding and idealism, as well as a willingness and need for deep intercultural exchange. This leads to a magical sense of community, to connections between like-minded people and to a kind of pre-selection. This is what increases the probability of meeting people with whom something more than friendship develops through a shared sense of belonging and often a shared philosophy of life.

As a platform to meet people in your own city or a means of finding a hang-out in the spirit of Tinder (as is increasingly the case), Couchsurfing in principle offers the opportunity for a similar intercultural experience without travelling. However, this inevitably means that Couchsurfing can be used like a dating portal—and it is widely used as such.

As I had been using Couchsurfing for a number of months, it was crucial for me to look forward to meeting the respective hosts as friends and to feel safe and welcome; otherwise it would be far too strenuous as a permanent form of travel. I therefore regularly invested whole days in the corresponding research and preparatory communication, wrote long personal letters and considered suitable gifts. I also avoided sending Couchsurfing requests to women I could imagine dating, because the couch is a temporary residence, a haven, your home.

Friends become Paypals
Couchsurfing and its modern successors

I love pho bo: fresh coriander, crisp bean sprouts, a bit of red chilli in steaming bowl of deliciousness. I'm having a farewell dinner with Lao, my host in Sydney. After just a few days, he feels like an old friend.

Lao is one of the Couchsurfing hosts who has left the most enduring and significant impressions on my life. After working in the corporate world for several years, he made a discovery. While sitting in a management meeting, he noticed how his thoughts and dreams had yet again wandered beyond the walls of the conference room and that only really a shadow of himself had remained in the chair.

It was time to go.

Now he works as an extreme sportsman and photographer. He has turned his apartment into a social hotspot where he takes in Couchsurfing and Airbnb guests, although he now only takes Couchsurfers when he's not booked out on Airbnb.

He is a well-read and experienced spiritual traveller. His philosophy of life can be summed up like this: Look around and try to find the colour blue. If you search conscientiously and with consideration, care and curiosity you're sure to find plenty.

Once you've finished, ask yourself how much green you noticed?

The questions you ask of life and what you look for determine what you will find.

International student and youth exchange programmes, voluntary service and platforms for organic farm work (e.g. WWOOF[22]) are now everywhere and allow thousands, perhaps millions of people to gain formative experiences in international understanding and intercultural learning. This is one of the great achievements of our time and a valuable part of the heritage of twentieth century cataclysms.

In this globalized world, intercultural skills have also acquired a high economic market value. They are constituent parts of a world that includes internships, studying abroad and "elective" migrants (expats) as well as the topic of refugees and their integration.

Couchsurfing itself has undergone a change that is still surprising for many "old" Couchsurfers. Sacrificing its non-profit status and the core element of unpaid services by moving to a commercial platform in 2011 caused the community to die within a few months. The magic vanished into thin air in no time at all. It was over. Couchsurfing was a community in spirit, an idealistic real utopia. The decision to sell data (e.g. profile content and images) and to restrict functionalities (especially with regard to local communities), resulted in a veritable exodus of Couchsurfers. This led to an even greater acceleration of trends in the direction of becoming a pure dating website and a provider of accommodation for freeloaders, which were already making waves in the community. The result was an erosion of the original idea behind Couchsurfing and a loss of cohesion among the community.

The basic features are still there for further wonderful experiences between individual hosts and Couchsurfers. I have continued to use Couchsurfing over the past few years, albeit with decreasing regularity. However, I too believe that the Couchsurfing of a community and local groups has all but ceased to exist.

The question arises as to whether this could have been prevented. Admittedly, this question is pointless insofar as the development has already taken place. However, given the wonderful experiences Couchsurfing has provided so many people, it is interesting to offer some final thoughts here. Perhaps we might gain some valuable insights for this and other communities.

Couchsurfing was on the verge of collapse when a serious database error occurred back in 2006. As time went by, huge growth led to one question arising with increasing regularity: could the requirements of such a large organisation actually have been maintained in the long term through a non-profit organisation and a very high proportion of voluntary work? From this perspective, it is possible to see the step towards commercialisation as a market necessity and to present this development as inevitable.

You could say the same of the increasing use of Couchsurfing for dating and freeloading as it became ever more popular. And yet the "seeds of Servas", of Luitweiler and Zamenhof, of the medical services that were the beginning of organisations such as the Red Cross and AFS, the spirit of international understanding and "holy" hospitality, were stifled by commercialisation. Was this too high a price? Would Couchsurfing have been marginalised over time as Servas was? Is this the price of enormous growth? What are the alternatives to commercialisation or is economic viability the only thing that makes survival possible?

Back to Lao. Airbnb has been even more consistent in its approach to the commercialisation of hospitality: you pay for "being a guest". The result is that it is inherently much more difficult (if not impossible) to establish the equality of host and guest as a basic prerequisite for the experience of genuine hospitality. The host is now a service provider and the guest is a customer. There are certain to be exceptions. There always are. But even with Airbnb, one experiences the fleetingness of authenticity, the impossibility of commercialising true (neighbourly) love. Economic potential has long since blurred the border between Airbnb and other platforms for holiday homes: the providers and places offered are often identical. Contact and exchange between the "host" and the "guest" is often limited to credit card or PayPal.

Airbnb Experiences is another approach to create greater closeness between travellers and the local population, and to make authenticity available as a commodity. I don't know whether to laugh or cry. Some might criticise a comparison between Laurie Lee being invited to a Spanish dinner on his trip[23] and paying someone via Airbnb to invite you to a typical paella. Is the latter merely a staged, Hollywood paella: a reproduction of one of the memes of the tourist market? A more positive take is that even the market has at least recognised the value of such experiences and that such experiences are more beneficial to both the service provider and the tourist than the package tour house fronts on the Spanish coast.

From a somewhat more detached perspective, the development of Couchsurfing can perhaps be compared to the early hitchhiker community. Back when there were just a few cars on the roads, hitchhiking was for a few years a symbol of freedom, trust and a euphoric community. Hitchhiking provided exciting and enriching encounters for both those who hitched and those who gave rides. For many they were an expression of an attitude to life and a philosophy of life. With the masses came change; euphoria gave way to mistrust. Today the attitude towards one's own car is one of "my home is my castle".

For me the Couchsurfing phenomenon was not just the basis of my journey around the world; it was how I met my wife: dancing cheek-to-cheek on a large open-air parquet wooden floor on a summer evening in Gorky Park. Fireworks over Moscow. Two hearts skipped a beat.

The stars of Shanghai

China

Pumping beats and porcelain faces
Through the night

The taxi drove up. Our eyes met. The bass was still pulsing through my veins. Tiredness and drink had thickened the flow of my thoughts to a sticky pomade.

Should I go with Lien? Behind me was Chen Lu, whose body was still imprinted on my skin from the closeness of our dancing. Even in the brash neon light of the street her eyes and lips had lost almost nothing of their seductive pull. Should I go with Chen Lu?

The proximity of a new naked body, another unknown place, a different bed, the smell of another unknown shower gel, the intimacy of another strange apartment?

A few stolen kisses and I jumped quickly into the taxi. The words "next time" fell from my lips. My thirst for adventure and novelty had long been satisfied. It was my own body that took me by the hand and led me home. Alone.

My plane had touched down on the runway of Shanghai Airport just a few hours before. I took the magnetic levitation train, the metro and then continued on foot, following Chinese hieroglyphs. After a short search I found my friend Matz's apartment. He lived in Pudong, in the middle of New Shanghai, a world of housing block canyons and churned-out residential areas that seemed to me to be a very futuristic vision of utopian conformity. A winter fog, thickened by the smoke and fumes of the metropolis, made the concrete mountains seem even more barren and soulless.

Matz and his Indonesian girlfriend lived in one of the residential areas that shot up out of the ground. Their heart-felt welcome and familiar faces warmed my mind and soul. We chatted a bit about our delicious food in a steaming noodle bar and then I was off on my way to meet Lien, sitting in taxi holding a scrap of paper with a scribbling of Chinese characters—the address of the bar where we were meeting.

The porcelain faces of advertisements flickered on the small screen in the front seat as we passed increasingly grim-looking high-rise districts outside. Suddenly we stopped abruptly in the middle of a particularly gloomy spot. It looked like a scene from a bad thriller or Mafia movie. I prepared myself for what might come. I had been looking at the driver a little suspiciously for minutes. Now he turned and offered me a dull but trusting smile. We had reached our goal.

I slowly climbed down the steps into the club and immediately found myself in another world. The pumping beats set my heart racing. The sea of ecstatic faces and enticing figures engulfed my senses. A radiant young Chinese woman came up to me and threw her arms around my neck. This obviously tipsy partygoer was Lien. She had invited me. By the time that our eyes met and I felt the warmth of her body in the near blackness of the room, it was clear that this would be an exciting night.

Lien then introduced me to her friend. Miga was even more enchanting and barely let go of me after a welcome kiss. It was as if I were in some kind of amazing dream.

It was only with some hesitation that I had left Matz. I'd actually only planned to have a quick drink and catch some sleep after the exhausting exertions of travelling. A cinematic episode unfolded.

Enter John: A tall, well-built Dutchman took the stage and introduced himself as Miga's boyfriend. After a few drinks, the four of us were in a taxi, heading to the next club. Lien, Miga and I in the back, John in the front. Miga kissed me unexpectedly and the taxi squealed to a halt in the middle of the street. John wanted a man-to-man fight and rolled up his sleeves, Miga jumped out of the car and wrapped herself around him to calm him down. I jumped back into the taxi, the door slammed behind me, and Lien and I raced on with another squeal of tyres. A thought raced through my head: "Whew, that was close!".

After another intermezzo in a smaller bar, we arrived at a rooftop club on Bund Park. It had a view of New Shanghai's skyline, which is probably the definitive symbol of New China. The atmosphere was much more exclusive. It was early morning and the party was raging. There were lots of expats and even more local beauties. The design of the club was modern and the huge building was filled with a spirit of mischievous fun. The floor vibrated with dancing feet. I began to feel and celebrate the optimism and dynamism of this rapidly growing city.

Party girl Lien introduced me to some other friends, and soon I was dancing in the middle of a big group. Chen Lu and I moved well together. Our bodies worked well together. We got closer. Lien saw her chance had slipped away. "It's late", she said. The taxi pulled up.

iPhones in the smog
Questioning China

Fog crawled slowly across the ground, hanging sluggishly between the prefabricated buildings. They say that in Shanghai you no longer see the stars at night. I saw people with face masks. Mao's slogans stared at me from gaudy posters in a propaganda museum. Ling, a writer I met via Couchsurfing was my intellectual guide. We talked for many hours about progress, the past, superstition, our dreams and our lives. Sometimes we talked in a Starbucks, sometimes over traditional dumplings, sometimes on the futuristic metro and sometimes on a trip to an old village with red lanterns. The conversation always revolved around similar questions:

"Is the dynamism of turbo-capitalism dissolving traditions in China too?"

"What does China bring to this brave new world? What has it lost?"

On the posters in the shopping malls and in the residential areas of the nouveau riche, everything was geared towards the individual, the consumer.

"Where is there still room for collectivity? Is China selling its soul? Will China conquer the world? At what cost?"

Ling lived alone. As did the thoughtful Yan-Yi, with whom I silently glided through the streets on my electric scooter. She was in marketing and was working on the messages her country wanted to use to present itself to the world as part of the Summer Olympics. You couldn't see anything from her twenty-third-floor apartment except concrete and smog.

Of course, these were always just subjective impressions, from the point of view of my experiences and the topics that were on my mind at the time. But I had the impression that in my search for the good life, communities and ways of life to refill the anonymity and atomisation of the modern world with love and humanity, I wouldn't find what I was looking for in east-coast urban China. The queues and crowds of the metro, the number of electronic devices to which people gifted their waking hours, cities in which the inhabitants can no longer see stars at night. Was it all worth it?

Then there were the monumental production facilities, a visit to which positively force upon you images from Charlie Chaplin's *Modern Times*. Aldous Huxley wrote his dystopian novel *Brave New World* shortly after seeing Billingham Chemical Plant and a visit to a Chinese factory provides similar inspiration.

Or as Ling put it: "Is the weary dejection and stupor on the faces of these factory workers not also reflected in the sheen of a new iPhone?"

The land of opportunity

Australia

The perfect job in the perfect city

Sydney

Is it really possible to walk out the front door, surf on your dream beach, earn good money while looking out on Sydney Harbour, have a delicious bowl of pho bo for lunch, go for a long run along the bays and beaches, and then hit a nice little bar where you can drink a sundowner with a delightful companion?

It was in Sydney. A natural harbour with a coastline almost 200 miles long and plenty of islands at its centre, the city has more than 70 beaches. There are a large number of national parks within day-tripping distance, you can see the Blue Mountains in the distance and the biggest ski resort in the southern hemisphere is just over 300 miles away.

It is also a multicultural city with the Mediterranean climate of Barcelona, a booming economy and—with a population of just 24 million on a land mass almost twice that of the 27 EU states—offers sufficient space and opportunities for everyone. In this respect it has a spirit that might be compared to that of the USA 150 years ago.

If you are—as I was—lucky enough to have a good friend who lives right on Bondi Beach and luckier enough to get a lucrative job near Sydney Harbour Bridge, it's also an almost unbeatable experience, at least for a working holiday.

There's another side to the story of course: more than 40 miles of sprawling suburbs, increasing commuting times, an obesity problem even greater than that of the USA[24] and a skin cancer epidemic.[25]

Local fruit and vegetable farms are also being ousted as a result of relentless urban expansion.

But back to the sunny side of life and the first perfect job of the trip.

I'd arrived down under just a few days before and my priority was to set off travelling. Having accompanied my friend Liliana (an ex-colleague from my time in Berlin) to the university where she was studying for her doctorate, boredom led me to log in to the student social networking site StudiVZ[26] for the first time in ages to see if there might be a group for working holidays in Australia.

As chance would have it, someone had just posted that they were urgently looking for German-speaking (could it have been any less believable?) backpackers for a construction job. The only conditions were the ability to start in two days' time and possession of a work permit. It turned out that I was able to complete the relevant training the following day. Two days later I was standing in front of a newly built high-rise north of Sydney Harbour Bridge together with a few other German-speaking backpackers and plumbers to be greeted by a German engineer.

We shot up to the sixtieth floor in a high-speed lift. Thankfully, the work was pretty simple. All that needed to be done was to remove the ceilings and then photograph and mark every single connector for the air-conditioning. The reason behind the work on this brand-new, as yet uninhabited high-rise was apparently water damage related to the air-conditioning system. This was leading to huge financial loses every day, as the building was ready for occupancy. As the actual technical inspection and validation had to be conducted by several German engineers, the idea was that all of us communicating in German only would guarantee efficient communication. It doesn't take much imagination to work out that there are an almost never-ending number of connectors in a huge high-rise. And so I had it made for weeks.

As Australian labour law stipulates that overtime and working on weekends and public holidays is generously remunerated, and as the client wanted the work done as quickly as possible, the job essentially financed my entire time in Australia. It was an unexpectedly ideal situation to be able to regard every subsequent job primarily as a bonus.

The best thing was that we had a great time. We'd shop for food at Aldi (these German supermarkets get everywhere), stick on some good music, enjoy the view of the harbour and exchange stories of the previous months, sometimes years, of travelling during the constant, monotonous, rather unchallenging work. We'd also make plans for the future:

"Kiwi season's coming up in New Zealand. We want to work as harvest helpers and then head over to the South Island."

"I'm in the northern hemisphere for the summer starting with forestry in Canada. Then it's down the Yukon in a canoe."

"Have any of you driven diggers in the gold mines over in Western Australia? Apparently it's not just the mine owners that earn a packet!"

Some of the other backpackers had been travelling for years. They were making use of Germany's various working holiday agreements with Australia, New Zealand and Canada. These deals allow young adults to discover new countries and meet new people in some of the most beautiful places on the planet, changing jobs every few months. It is for many the time of their lives and an experience they can draw on forever.[27]

If work or the gorgeous view got too boring, it helped that there was usually a barbecue, a date or a night out with friends to look forward to. And, of course, there was also the next trip and the next couch to be planned.

Australia was the biggest surprise on my journey around the world. It had never had that much of a pull for me. Instead it was the cultures of South and Central America, Africa and Asia that had always captured my imagination. I had always found the other and the exotic more beguiling—after all, I was looking for something new, the unknown and adventure. From what I had read and heard from friends and acquaintances, Australia seemed to be a huge desert with a few cities vaguely resembling US metropolises and an otherwise mainly British influence, only with more sun and as a result more skin cancer. I had been told it was a superficial country with no politics and no culture, just barbecues and sport, a party Mecca for gap year kids from the UK with a few pretty bits of coral in the water. In short, a low-brow destination.

However, against all my expectations, the three or so months I was there were among the most intense, enjoyable and formative of the time I spent travelling and of my entire life. Sydney took its place right up there on my list of places to move to. The country I got to know was full of optimism with a high standard of living and an inviting work/life balance. I discovered alternative forms of living together and completely new spiritual dimensions both in myself and in life.

I have never felt so free before or since.

Lazing in the Outback
Freedom

The occasional handful of sand or tumbleweed blown across the path by the wind. Other than that, complete silence. Heat.

I moved slowly, ponderously towards one of the few houses to look at the job listings. Social worker on an Aboriginal reserve? Tour guide for Uluru? A stint at a roadhouse?

The Aborigines fascinated me to at least the same degree as the Fulani in the north of Ghana. The feeling I had was an indescribable sense of another world, another time. It was a feeling of excitement, somehow full of longing and adventure. The idea of spending a couple of months in close contact with Aborigines was hugely appealing to me. They were different. I really wanted to learn from them, to talk with them. About dreaming tracks. About modern times. About life.

There was also the power and infinite nature of the place. The rich red of the Outback, the soft, mild, captivating turquoise of the sky in the morning. Thousands of miles of desert in every direction. The sandy earth, breathing out the peace of millions of undisturbed years.

Nowhere did I experience this energy more powerfully than at Uluru. This monolith existed long before life on land. It existed in the time of the first palaeocontinent. Its unique form has defied the erosion of hundreds of millions of years. Never before have I had such a mystical experience as when the first rays of the sun set the mountain flanks aglow.

Perhaps I should become a tour guide. My tour of Uluru had been amazing. Geoff, our guide, had managed to give us a feel for the magic of the place, to enchant us. He had taught us humility towards and respect for the Earth. He had also imbued in us a fascination for the Aboriginal way of life and Aboriginal wisdom. Wide-eyed amazement.

Did I want to experience again the Milky Way in the desert's nocturnal firmament, to share it with others, to share it with other travellers instead of working with the Aborigines?

Or did I want the lethargy of a roadhouse? That also had its appeal. A life like the opening scene from *Once Upon a Time in the West*: doing nothing more than dozing in the languid hum of a fan, any test of strength limited to the occasional swat at a fly. Watching a car appear on the horizon a couple of times a day, taking the customers' money and returning to my snooze.

Or did I simply want to dream?

Freedom. Freedom to stay here a while. To go north, south, east or west. Or to lie down on the ground and do nothing.

Better living through communality

Harvest helpers in Riverland

The low tones of the didgeridoo flew towards the setting sun. The rays became ever more mellow and the lengthening shadows lent an increasingly gentle nature to the landscape, softening the brittleness of the scorched day.

I loved every one of them somehow. Keita, who was playing the didgeridoo. Paavo, who was drumming with his broad, ice-hockey-player's back to me. Ito, who was dozing in the hammock. Knut and Takiito, who were up to some shenanigans in the rowing boot. And all the others who were simply part of the big family sharing this moment of harmony. And was all happening   in   this   wonderful   place.

Having set out from our "farm" in the morning to spend the day mucking about, in the sauna, swimming, and eating and drinking on the houseboat, we were enjoying a fantastic Sunday outing as a family. "Farm" is most definitely an inadequate term for something that is difficult to describe in words. Artistic tree houses, a colourful tepee with a metal horse, a camper van, a tennis court, an ultimate frisbee field, various lounge areas, a sauna, a beautiful pool, countless buddhas, sculptures, swings, and a main house with a kitchen and a party barn. An artwork. A masterpiece. An oasis.

A commune. Located somewhere on the edge of the Outback, a river meant there was fertile soil nearby, on which grew grapes, oranges, and plenty of other fruit and vegetables. The story goes that it was a Norwegian who started this communal living project for international harvest workers in South Australia's Riverland.

Working days typically began before daybreak so that we could complete the day's labour before the brutal midday sun. Despite the limited working hours and our limited skills, we were able to earn a quite respectable amount of money. Being competitive, I began to challenge others, mainly the stoic Koreans and Japanese, who were sometimes here for many months so that they could save up a tidy sum. Our work was usually followed by very long, idle afternoons, during which almost everything you can image in such a scenario happened: snoozing, sport, cooking together, playing music, juggling, out-of-control parties, evenings in the pool and sauna, intrigues, theft, and of course plenty of lusting and loving.

The lightness of being
Underwater at the Great Barrier Reef

Our yacht had laid anchor at an isolated island and using just a simple snorkel and mask I was able to enter an unknown world just a few inches below the surface.

An almost weightless lightness of being. Below me sprawled a world of coral and sponge in gentle, fluid, perpetual movement, presenting new images ad infinitum. Colourful fish glided and flitted in the space between. Most appeared not to notice me at all. One or two nibbled at me inquisitively or stared, saucer-eyed, into my goggles. The turtles that floated majestically by were more sublime creatures.

Yet again, I was in love with life.

As so often on my travels, I was startled by the beauty. The element of surprise made the impact even greater, as I was simply going with the flow of things. Although I occasionally planned a particular change of direction, I then let myself be carried by the swell of happenings. The only fixed elements were a flexible ticket that could be changed at any time and expired within a year. Everything else happened of its own accord and quite often by chance.

It was a bit like summer in Berlin: hitting the town with friends in one of the city's hipper areas on a warm summer night, not knowing where we would end up, what we were doing or with whom we would wake up. It was the feeling of being drunk on bravado and high spirits, spurred on by the summer air and young, expectant faces. Gliding through the night, the music and laughter that surrounded us, kind of crowdsurfing on euphoria and freedom and becoming almost weightless.

Seeing life in perspective

A meditation retreat in the Blue Mountains

Into the blue wide open
Setting off and settling in

Blue sky above us, we travelled past endless forest slopes on the way towards the glimmering ocean horizon. Music blasted out of the speakers. Happiness and hunger for life radiated from our very beings.

We felt so light, so blessed, so pure. Life seemed so full of promise and wonder.

Ten days before, the train had rattled and jolted its way deeper and deeper into the expanse of the Blue Mountains. My growing sense of keen curiosity was mixed with a pinch of scepticism and uncertainty—all wrapped up in a tranquil resignation to fate and my prevailing happy-go-lucky world-traveller mood.

The train journey took me to a Vipassana retreat surrounded by a grove of eucalyptus trees. The first cool nights had begun to descend upon the area: the Blue Mountains, on the outskirts of Greater Sydney.

One of the main goals of my trip had been to connect more intensively with spirituality and faith, and to fathom their significance for the history and diverse cultures of mankind, as well as for myself. Discovering more about the power and significance of meditation through personal experience was a tangible step in this direction. Why are meditation techniques so central to different cultures? What are the essential experiences and functions of meditation? Could mediation function as a kind of 'stargate' to other spiritual dimensions? Would I be able to access these?

I wanted to find out.

Noble silence and equanimity
The principles of the retreat

Vipassana is a meditation technique.[28]

Its efficacy comes from practising the technique. Vipassana is independent of belief and religion; it is perhaps better categorised as an art of mind training.

As with many important things in life, the basic principles of the retreat are very simple:

Ten days of "noble silence"—no communication, verbal or non-verbal.

Extremely minimalist, ascetic, vegetarian nutrition (a light breakfast, a light lunch and a piece of fruit in the afternoon)

Most of the day spent in sitting meditation, sometimes in a group, sometimes alone.

A selection of group meditations begins with short explanations (lasting a few minutes) to teach the technique. The first days involve teaching a mind-focusing technique (Samatha), followed by the actual Vipassana technique. Samatha is an observation of your breathing, while Vipassana is a continuous observation of the sensations on your skin.

The basic principle and goal of observing both your breathing and the sensations on your skin is equanimity. The aim is to observe everything, to avoid judgement and to be aware of the transient nature of things, be it quick or slow breathing, the coolness of the air you breathe in or the warmth of the air you breathe out, a mild prickly feeling or an intense itchiness. As being in the present is a precondition of observation, the first thing to be taught is the complementary technique of focusing and regathering thoughts whenever they begin to wander using Samatha.

That's all there is to it. For many people, these few basic principles create an extraordinary and often fundamentally moving experience. For some it is the starting point for a lifetime of practising the technique.

The mosaic of life
The experience of meditation

How can such simple rules have such a transformative effect?

First of all, at its root, the rule of silence means exactly that: silence. It is the suspension, the slow ebb, of constant overstimulation. Combined with a concentrated focus on your own breathing, this creates a significant awareness of your body. In the first few days I also genuinely had the feeling that I was becoming increasingly more perceptive, until I felt that I consisted entirely of perception. I observed my breathing and my body, but increasingly felt a state of pure observation. I felt that I could decide how and when I reacted to an itch on my cheek or pins and needles in my leg. This was a new sensory experience and filled me with much peace, with the result that I could feel my mental strength and self-determination increasing.

But these first few days were above all difficult. They were boring. I had gone from the opulence and inebriation of travelling around the world to monastic asceticism. On many occasions I stood at the entrance to the compound, contemplating whether I should simply open the gate and leave. One of the initial uses to which I put my new mental sharpness and intensity of thoughts and memories was to experience a kind of virtual reality of particularly pleasant experiences, especially certain moments of sensual and erotic adventure. It was a pretty fantastic experience to be honest, but it was still a far cry from the intensity of feeling that I was to experience later.

Ultimately, what kept me going in the first few days was the ethos of the *Karate Kid* films of my youth: to live the strictly disciplined life of a monk for at least these ten days and to come out of it with increased inner strength. It was a playful, childlike thought that had a major effect.

It takes a certain ethos to wake up in complete darkness at 5:30 a.m. to the sound of a gong in the bracing morning air of the Blue Mountains and shuffle, lulled by the blanket wrapped around you, to the meditation hall in order to attempt to maintain concentration with aching limbs, keep your head upright and maintain the necessary tension to avoid being overcome by sleep.

I was very lucky that although the atmosphere of the retreat was very subdued and every-man-for-himself, there was something powerful and positive in the air surrounding the eucalyptus trees. There was an atmosphere of self-imposed asceticism, testing one's own courage and austerity for the sake of self-realisation, clarity and creativity, as well as a certain sense of community and a growing familiarity.

After I had traversed the low point at the beginning of the actual Vipassana meditation, an increasingly deep-seated sense of peace and a warm sense of harmony began to spread throughout my body. When my thoughts began to wander, I was taken back in time to my early childhood. On these journeys, the people, my feelings and decisions were as close as in the actual situations themselves. The only difference was that I was now a meek observer. Slowly, the mosaic of my life began to form a cohesive whole. Although this mosaic was not without its starkly juxtaposed sections, there were constant key tones that via various changes in colour and structure presented a fundamental spectrum in which I met myself with tender love.

With this harmony came a deep gratefulness and loving benevolence towards the others who had enriched my life. Going against the strict rules forbidding any kind of record, I began to make an increasingly long list of people I wanted to thank.

It was a further development that had perhaps the biggest direct and tangible effect on my life after the retreat: a map of my life began to crystallise out of the growing connection to my previous life, including moments of happiness and difficult times. On this map, my various worries, desires, fears, goals, problems and aspirations were organised in such a clear, natural manner that many decisions appeared completely obvious and trivial. Many long-fostered beliefs and apparent problems were automatically resolved in this new clarity, and I wrote down a number of resolutions, concrete decisions and specific measures that had become self-evident no-brainers.

The last day of the Vipassana retreat was a real highlight. We dubbed it "Airbag Day". In order to achieve a smoother transition from sensory asceticism to the overflowing stream of life outside the meditation centre and allow an exchange of experiences between the participants, the principle of noble peace was, with the exception of seated meditation sessions, repealed for this final day. And what a cascade of conversation, laughter and pure joy it let loose. There was an unbelievable feeling of having "returned to life" and of valuing the gift of speech and the various forms of non-verbal communication more than perhaps ever before. The once reserved, in some cases po-faced, participants suddenly turned into radiant sources of love and sympathy—rarely have I felt such an ecstasy for being human. And naturally there was also a uniting feeling of pride and relief to have seen it out.

As luck would have it, I got to know some fantastic people (ranging from managers to magicians and from backpackers to successful pop musicians) and was able to spend a great deal of time with several of them later.

We really couldn't and didn't want to stop smiling, laughing, sharing all the harmony and joy, expressing ecstatic feelings of affection for the others.

We had our blankets wrapped around us. Again. We were sitting in an uncomfortable position and would be for the next two hours. Again. We tried to concentrate and immerse ourselves in our thoughts. Suddenly, there was a little parp from somewhere within the room. It wasn't the first time with the wholefood, vegetarian diet. A few moments passed, perhaps a few minutes, and there was another parp from another corner of the room. This time, it was impossible to suppress the sniggering that followed. Although discipline and severity, the ethos of the Karate Kid, were victorious, it was merely the calm before the storm. The first participants stood up and quickly left the room. Then the next few rushed out, barely able to control their laughter. After a few seconds, I fell victim to it too and joined the unfettered guffawing to lie joyfully in the arms of the others.

Spiritual pragmatism and universal ethics

Vipassana meditation and our time

While researching Vipassana in German, I constantly encountered the term "*Befreiungspragmatismus*" ("a practical approach to freedom"), which I found apt. It refers to freedom in the here and now. Vipassana is a mind-training technique, an art in the sense of a craft, like a martial art or an art of living.[29]

The word "Vipassana" occurs regularly in the Buddhist teaching language of Pali and (depending on etymological interpretation) can be expressed in English as to "see into", "see through" or "see in a special way" in the sense of "insight". These are, however, mere words, to which one should not seek too much attachment.

Unavoidably, there are very different views and interpretations of the various texts and traditions of Buddhism. This is an inherent part of Buddhism, as the religion came into being around 2500 years ago, the historical Buddha appears not to have written anything and every tradition changes each time it is passed on or translated. It is one of the fundamental challenges faced by researchers in the subjects of history, philosophy and theology.

There is a consensus that the techniques of mindfulness meditation were central to the teaching and practice of Buddhism. And it is because of the importance of mindfulness meditation that we owe a debt of gratitude to Buddhist traditions for their many valuable texts, ideas and techniques.

I regard Buddhism as a philosophy of life with a strong focus on action. I see it as a belief only in the sense that it assumes a system of universal ethics or a law of nature.

Anyone can become a buddha and experience enlightenment. I interpret this as a state of permanent connection to the essence of love and belonging of all being, including the law of nature. The pragmatic nature of Buddhism also means that this awareness of practical living in the moment entails the ability to act ethically and with love, as one has the necessary clarity of vision. Clarity means seeing through and overcoming the perpetual state of entrapment and the unremitting evaluation of things that are in any case ephemeral.

According to Goenka, upon whose teachings the meditation I practised was based, the historical Jesus and Mohammed were buddhas and anyone who identifies as a Christian or Muslim can express their religion by putting the ethics of these historical persons into practice in life to achieve enlightenment.

When Buddhism was later institutionalised, some aspects of the simple nature of its fundamental orientation were changed. If one wants to combine a philosophy of life or belief with institutions and power, a teaching that is completely oriented towards the individual and complete independence is largely useless. Monasteries and clerics require a monopoly on the path to freedom or paradise to justify their existence, and similarly, huge state structures have always used a form of institutionalised spirituality for cohesion.

Vipassana seems to have captured the contemporary mood. Despite the ambitious expansion of Vipassana meditation centres throughout the entire world, they are booked out, often months in advance.

Vipassana has, as mindfulness training, now been medically and empirically confirmed as having a positive effect on stress reduction, and programmes such as mindfulness-based stress reduction (MBSR) are increasingly popular.

In a time of constant sensory overload and a world of 24/7 online availability, actively doing nothing is both an oasis and a source of deep insight and harmony.

Rainbows and sheep

New Zealand

Snow. Fervent bellowing. Scantily clad rugby players scrabbled through the sludge. Anna, my Couchsurfing host, had wanted to share with me an experience of great cultural significance in New Zealand. It is full of tradition and power. The players are like warriors. Rugby is also a force for integration and national identity in this country. This is sport at its best. Native and non-native New Zealanders stand literally shoulder to shoulder, pushing in the same direction.

Nevertheless, it was early winter and it was bitingly cold in Christchurch. As my journey around the world has largely followed the summer, I was rather ill-prepared for this cold snap. I was still high on the mild, sunny, late-summer weather of Sydney, the manifold melodies of laughter and the smiles of friends I had come to love. I could still feel the hugs and tears of the intensely warm farewell. As a result, the sleet, the small-town smell of stadium hot dogs and the cold, wet weather really hit hard.

I had been staying with my close friend and dream woman, Mia, and had crawled out of bed early in the morning, still feeling the euphoria and exuberance of a fantastic long night of dancing with my dearest friends, those who had brought so much richness to my life down under. I'd taken the No. 400 bus to the airport again and said goodbye to the eucalyptus trees that I'd learnt to love. But this time I was off to catch an international flight, not a domestic one.

There's no feeling quite like thinking you're on the opposite side of the world and then flying to a country even further away. The combination of excitement and curiosity at the unknown, at a new world, arose again and blended with a feeling of "Why keep moving when it's so brilliant here?" In this case, I could take solace in the fact that I planned to return. It made the goodbye less stark; the door was open. The anticipation of seeing my friends again and the hugs upon my return didn't feel too far away. In fact, they felt very real.

I was back above the clouds, airborne again. The interesting thing is that even when I write "goodbye" or "farewell", I am aware that although time and time again I held on to fond memories and had the wonderful feeling of "This is the way it is the way it's meant to be", I still felt as if I were on a mission. I arrived at each new place ready to give it 100 percent, even when my stay was going to be short. Any thoughts of the future or past existed only as part of the immediate experience.

An attractive young woman was sitting next to me on the plane. It's a rare occurrence: the stuff of dreams, really. She had a positive, open, inviting aura and it didn't take long before we started talking. It couldn't have gone better in my dreams. Melinda was returning from several months of backpacking. She was a Couchsurfer.

"You know what? Stop by our farm. We've got a little holiday house. You can stay as long as you like." It wasn't long before I was invited to her parents' farm. At a later point on my New Zealand trip I took up residence on their farm in by far my swankiest "couch": an idyllic hut, surrounded by woods and meadows.

"Welcome to New Zealand. It's great to see you!" Anna was waiting at the airport with open arms and a greeting that couldn't have been more heartfelt had I been friend or family.

New Zealand. I had the feeling and the certainty of being far away. I was in the middle of nowhere, on the other side of the world. I was in a good place.

I loved New Zealand from the very beginning and saw it in permanent panorama. It was picture-postcard perfection everywhere I looked, especially on the South Island. At first sight, New Zealand offers similar elements of landscape to Central and Northern Europe, only in aesthetic excellence: gentle, rolling hills, rainbows, snow-capped summits, bays. Even the sheep somehow appeared even whiter and woollier. The landscapes merged into one another. There were almost no houses and even less evidence of urban life. A place to stay for a while. Or for longer. Just the right place to take a deep breath at the mid-point of my round-the-world trip.

Joshua, one of my Couchsurfing hosts, was working on a farm. Situated in an idyllic remote valley, deep green meadows rolled down the undulating hills that surrounded this lovely little plot of land. The landscape was speckled with white splashes of sheep. Here and there a horse grazed in a paddock. A few cows feasted on the lush grass of the level ground. A stream snaked its way between the hills to flow into the sea next to a sandy beach further up. I watched in near incredulity as I saw at first heads, then whole seal bodies splashing in the shallow waters of the bay.

Otherwise it was completely calm. The only movement appeared to be the slowly wandering shadows of the hilltops and the chewing motion of the sheep.

Joshua had been given sole custody of the farm for a few days. He was a travelling farmer, so to speak, and knew his way around from his work somewhere in the rural USA. Dusk marked the end of his exhausting working day. It had begun at dawn and had entailed several ascents and descents of the slopes in order to feed the livestock, put up fences and do all kinds of other small jobs with lots to carry.

I listened to his descriptions of working life in this distant country. Like an old storyteller, he recounted tales of stubborn sheep and insatiable cows.

"Joshua, how come you have to keep putting up new fences?", I asked him while we lay in the steaming jacuzzi, looking out at the sea.

"There are some rules of thumb as to how much land a sheep grazes each day", he answered. "I have to keep marking out new areas so that the animals have enough to eat and graze the fields equally." He raised his glass. "I'm really glad you made it over to find me in this remote corner of the world. It can be pretty lonely here with just the cows and sheep." His thoughtful gaze drifted across the surrounding landscape. "I'll never cease to be enchanted by the beauty and peace of this little spot."

His calm, melodic voice, a cold beer and the crisp coming of the night helped me drift slowly into tranquil tiredness. We put the cover on the jacuzzi and put out the lights. Then I snuggled under a warm blanket and sank into a deep sleep.

Everyone I met through Couchsurfing in New Zealand had an interesting story about how they had ended up there and what they were up to. A yoga and meditation centre combined with an eco-resort? A government-sponsored qualification as an adventure tourism guide on the South Island, including such arduous-sounding training as fjord-kayaking and parachuting?

New Zealand is a land of truly fabulous and fantastic qualities.

And yet, precisely because of this I was surprised by a creeping feeling inside me, a kind of instinct. The hilly countryside with its nestlike valleys, the lush greenery, the cows, the horses, the brisk autumnal feel: was this peaceful, inspiring feeling in this remote place partly due to the fact that it was a little bit like it was "at home"?

I hadn't quite learnt to trust my instinct. Everywhere was certainly much less densely populated and simply beautiful, especially with the sea. Nevertheless, I took this feeling with me and discovered it again while jogging past farms and along oak- and beech-lined lanes "at home" in Germany after long Caribbean summers. Despite being as fleeting as the scent of a pretty woman passing by and as shy as a fawn in the twilight, the feeling of being at home is still deeply moving whenever it spreads through me.

The appeal of dreams

USA

The goldrush and the matrix

Los Angeles

After taking a deep breath in the land of the long white cloud (the Māori name for New Zealand) I was faced with a long flight across the Pacific and the international date line: Auckland to Los Angeles. This entailed another very stark contrast: late autumn in the lush, green landscape of tranquil, peaceful New Zealand, a country in which sheep outnumber humans by ten to one, and summer in the hot, smoggy metropolis of Los Angeles with its vast hinterland of deserts.

I find attempting to conceive this contrast somewhat comparable to the limits of the human capacity to conceive quantum mechanics or astronomy. Although it is a logical and indisputable fact that the seasons are the opposite way around in the northern and southern hemispheres, I still can't really get my head around it. I can't imagine the summer when it's winter in Germany and vice versa. Even watching a live stream of the Australian Open being played in the scorching heat of January doesn't help me if I'm lounging about in the candlelight, curled up in a thick fleece pullover.

I see Los Angeles (Hollywood itself, the villas of Malibu and Orange County, and the boulevards of Beverly Hills) as akin to the centre of the matrix of the modern world, even if the Bay Area (which includes the Apples, Googles, Facebooks and Teslas of Silicon Valley) has become a formidable challenger to LA's Dream Factory.

LA's location alone makes it quite some place to live! It has 263-day-a-year sunshine; beautiful, warm beaches; the fruit farms of Central Valley; and the cool, green mountains of Sierra Nevada just a few hours away. But I'm not the first to have recognised this: 40 million people now live there and California is the largest economy in the world after the USA, Japan, China and Germany. Back in 1900, the population was just one million. By 1950, it had grown to ten million. The Gold Rush of 1850 (at which time the population was just 100,000) has not stopped.

My hub for North and Central America was Venice, where I stayed on the couch of a diminutive dominatrix and a banker. Both surfing-mad, they were always ready to drive for several hours in search of the perfect wave given the right weather conditions. The dominatrix's most regular clients were the super-rich and their offspring. Her job entailed taking such people on creative paths to discover and go beyond their limits. The couple were extremely relaxed, generous hosts who guaranteed good conversation and unusual places to experience the local nightlife.

In one of the clubs, I met an attractive Mexican woman who took me on a trip in her convertible and invited me to a wedding in Mexico. I met Miss Salsa at a street salsa event in Santa Monica and paddled with her through Huntington Harbour, a pompous area full of yachts and villas. I had magic mushrooms thrown at me at a downtown rooftop bar and experienced an atmosphere at an LA reggae club with marijuana smoke so thick I could have used it as a Rastafarian magic carpet. The rest of my time was spent doing Vegas, Yosemite, the Grand Canyon, rafting, etc. In short, I did what people do on the (south-)west coast.

The land of hope
New York

"Electrifying" best describes the feeling that I still get every time I step onto the subway after arriving at JFK.

If LA is the Dream Factory at the centre of the matrix, the svengali for the fantasies of millions, then I see New York as the real capital, the epicentre of the modern era. If you include the wider area of Washington and Boston, then it is a melting pot, a control room, a financial, scientific and cultural epicentre, whose reverberations can be felt throughout almost the entire world.

As with many new cities, I first got to know New York by discovering it on long walks, illuminating jogging routes and through my many Couchsurfing contacts. These included a skater and her Latino model boyfriend who conveniently lived in the W on Times Square. The location and free drinks made it an ideal starting point for a long night out in New York. Other Couchsurfing contacts included the hundreds who turned up to a party that ended with romantic (sometimes slightly naughty) dares as the sun rose on the waterfront.

For a long time, New York was above all a symbol of hope for millions of people. I was particularly touched by the descriptions of the mainly European immigrants waiting to enter at the docks near the Statue of Liberty: this hope of a new, better world, of a land of freedom and human rights, peace and prosperity, of the American Dream. All these people who brought these hopes from their various countries, not in the form of modest belongings, but in their hearts. And how often was it precisely such a positive expectation that first created what people had set out to find?

A considerably more profane example involves asking how many people went to Berlin, as I did, to find an experimental, dynamic, retro-style culture, most of which was only created by those who moved there with precisely those expectations?

Where is the New York of today, our "new world", our land of hope?

The limits of dreams and prosperity
Searching in the labyrinth of the modern age

I and many others (particularly those in "post-industrial service societies") increasingly regard the USA—the US model of society and life, the fabricated dreams of LA, the paradigms of growth and consumerism, the glorification of the self-made man— as less attractive, less worthy of emulation and less worthy of praise.

There are the widely discussed topics of the limits of growth, limited resources, the trashing of the world, climate change and the mass extinction of species. There is also an increasing awareness of ethical issues, particularly industrial livestock farming.

Even though the popular and equally one-sided indicators of growth and "wealth" tell another story, it is above all increasingly clear that in these times of industrial-scale human living, many people's lives are becoming poorer, particularly with regard to community and the feeling of belonging and connectedness. And this is leading to more and more people lagging behind on an emotional and mental level. Or as a US study puts it:

We may be materially richer than in the past. But with atrophied social capabilities, with a diminished sense of belonging to something greater than ourselves, and with less security in our family life, we are much poorer for doing less together.[30]

Some days, my primary interactions are with strangers in metal boxes (cars), I spend the bulk of my working day with Outlook, PowerPoint, Teams and on the phone. On such days, there is greater physical intimacy at a café or the gym, but also greater emotional distance and anonymity. If I then return to an apartment where contact is generally limited to neighbours' complaints about noise, the constant human distance becomes a bit too much. The result is that I feel like I'm light years away from fulfilling my basic social needs at that moment.

For the vast majority of our evolutionary history, it was normal to live together in small groups and tribes where everyone knew each other and no-one was a stranger. Today we as individuals are often part of an anonymous mass in which everyone or almost everyone is a stranger. "Stranger" was once almost always synonymous with "enemy". I believe that suddenly spending large parts of our life in such an environment tends to confuse our instincts more than we are aware of and more than we care to admit.

When you do interact, there are often designated roles set by hierarchies and anonymous protocols. This is true whether you are at work, out shopping, at a yoga course or at your local restaurant.

If we also take into account the constant sensory overload, it is hardly surprising that the beast in us is spooked and reacts angrily when we return to our tiny concrete boxes.

I certainly do not at any time soon expect to be surrounded by people dancing the merengue, lying permanently in one another's arms and simply living for the moment. I have even less expectation that small rural or perhaps nomadic groups will suddenly constitute a destabilising force in the hills of Central Germany as part of a back-to-nature or back-to-the-roots movement.

But even if the subjects surrounding the atomisation and anonymisation of modern consumer society are not new, countermeasures have until now primarily focused on individual transformation. We try to adapt to the paradigms of growth and consumerism instead of questioning them or trying to change them.

Psychology in the popular-science sense of self-help and positive thinking, as well as coaching and therapy, is booming. We seek fulfilment (yoga, searching for spiritual meaning, the perfect job and partner) in the individual sphere and in romantic relationships as a couple.

What if the land of hope lies somewhere else completely, perhaps somewhere entirely unexpected?

Maslow's pyramid and happiness
Belonging as true wealth

Almost a century ago, the eminent psychologist Abraham Maslow proposed a hierarchy of needs, presented as a pyramid. In the meantime, there have been some studies to test this theory empirically and to develop it on the basis of more recent findings in developmental biology and psychology. Some particularly exciting questions include whether there is a hierarchy at all, whether it varies according to situation, culture and phase of life, and what exactly the connection between and mutual contingency of these needs looks like.

The high importance of social bonding seems beyond question and as fundamental as basic biological needs. It also seems far more crucial for physical and psychological well-being than status and self-realisation.[31]

The results of a Harvard study, which achieved popularity primarily through a TED talk entitled "Harvard study, almost 80 years old, has proven that embracing community helps us live longer, and be happier"[32] say everything that needs to be said about the importance of resilient social relationships. This study has been running for more than 80 years and follows people of various social status throughout their lives. The main aim is to identify the factors that are most likely to predict the health and happiness (both physical and psychological) of participants in subsequent years.

The conclusion drawn was as follows: Close relationships, more than money or fame, are what keep people happy throughout their lives, the study revealed. Those ties protect people from life's discontents, help to delay mental and physical decline, and are better predictors of long and happy lives than social class, IQ, or even genes.[33]

So more than anything else, it is close social relationships that make us happy in the long term. It's not status symbols, a school-leaving certificate, an SUV or a Harvard education. And it's not the self-promotion and self-realisation that are the focus of so much attention today. It's not 10,000 followers on Instagram and it's not a single-figure golf handicap.

I regard many cultures and countries as richer than those countries which anthropologist Jared Diamond has christened WEIRD (Western, educated, industrialised, rich and democratic).[34]

Resilient social connections are the true wealth.

In the land of lust for life

See you in Colombia

The only risk is wanting to stay
Colombia

A Caribbean coast with dream beaches, well-preserved colonial towns and remote islands, tropical rainforest in the Amazon, glaciers and volcanos, deserts, a Pacific coast with whales and an economic centre of highlands with a moderate to mild climate and a slightly Central-European landscape. Colombia has almost every climatic zone, which means that it also has an almost unimaginable wealth of flora and biodiversity. It impressed Humboldt when he came to Colombia from Venezuela on his South American expedition. It also contributed to his theories of nature, which provided a central basis for various modern sciences, including ecology and the environmental protection movement.[35]

Colombia has the largest population in Latin America after Brazil (at 49 million, it is slightly more than that of Spain, on an area twice the size). It is also very diverse in ethnic terms. The majority of the population are of mixed European and indigenous descent, almost a third are direct descendants of European colonists, and a large proportion are of mixed European and African descent. There is of course also every other kind of permutation possible; in short, it is a very colourful mix.

The most important difference to most other countries in Latin America is the decentralised system of cities. In addition to Bogotá, a metropolis with a population of eight million, there are many other regional cities with populations of over a million, including Medellín, Cali, Barranquilla and Cartagena de Indias.

To most people, Colombia is probably still best known for its long history with armed conflict and drug cartels. It is an image that continues to be reproduced and marketed by Hollywood and others.

The age of the big drug cartels is now old history; the armed conflict has ended and the country is one of the most hyped economic locations in the world.

The pop superstar Shakira, the singer Juanes, the footballer James Rodríguez, the cyclist Nairo Quintana and an increasing number of others offer Colombia a different kind of international publicity. In contrast to other countries on the continent, it is not yet part of the tourist mainstream and is still full of off-radar wonders and rarely visited areas. It is also largely full of people who still greet guests with open arms, take them to their bosom and do not regard them first and foremost in economic terms, as walking cash points. Some travellers have apparently stayed longer, which is in keeping with an old slogan used by Colombia's tourism board: "The only risk is wanting to stay."

The little coral of stone
Cartagena de Indias

Both before and during my travels, several people predicted where I would feel most at home with the words "see you in Colombia". What did it for me and the things I've raved about since were the warmth and cheerfulness, the expression of joy and enthusiasm, the irresistibly lively music and expression of the people's lust for life through their exuberant dancing.

Ghana, South Africa and the many Brazilian acquaintances I had made on a long trip to Argentina had set a similar longing resonating in me. They had awakened my enthusiasm and admiration, and had exerted a great pull on me through their lightness of being and expressiveness. Even in Berlin I had felt like a family in my Latino circle of friends. I had lived, laughed and loved with Colombians, and so it was natural that my trip around the world would lead me to Colombia.

The route initially took me to Cartagena and the Caribbean coast, then Cali (the heartland of salsa) and finally to the highland capital of Bogotá at 2,640 metres above sea level. Then it was back to New York via Cartagena. At least that was the plan.

Cartagena is lovingly referred to by the locals using the typical Spanish diminutive as *el corralito de piedra* (the little coral of stone). Many travellers have been very taken with the place and it is now one of the most visited cities in Latin America.[36] Comprising several islands and peninsulas and with a spectacular, well-preserved colonial Old Town, the city centre is a real treasure. Just 30 minutes away by boat in the Caribbean Sea are several islands. They are perfect for diving and for revelling on the idyllic white sands and in the turquoise waters. There is more than enough to attract a wide range of tourists. In addition to the Old Town's exquisite boutique hotels there is a headland with two Miami-style districts that feature towering modern apartment blocks and huge hotels. On top of this, there are over 150 cruise ships, which unload hordes of people to stream through the alleyways of the historic centre on an almost daily basis.

Here too, Couchsurfing was my key to a colourful bouquet of acquaintances and I had cheerful companionship whenever I wanted. The very active international backpacker scene was another aspect that guaranteed a diverse social life. There were also sweet mangoes and delicious guava juice, coconut rice (my favourite) and long Caribbean nights with fantastic live music. It was a place to stay and enjoy for a while.

Cali felt like the dodgiest city I visited on my travels, but even there I had an excellent host. He had just taken in an entire busload of Couchsurfers for the annual salsa festival, most of them Colombians. The evenings were legendary and everyone was wet through with sweat and ecstatically happy after the long nights of dancing.

I felt like part of a big family with the very active Couchsurfing community in Bogotá and enjoyed a group connection and affection that I have rarely experienced. It was a never-ending flood of laughter, playfulness and dancing, lots of bodily contact and exchanges that ranged from superfluous small talk to deep philosophical conversations. It was a unique potpourri of ambitious, inquisitive, adventurous, idealistic young people: Couchsurfing at its best.

One evening, we went to an area with lots of homeless people so as to bring some joy to a few other people with some delicious goodies before the party. This was a regular Couchsurfing event. All of a sudden, the earth shook and a thunderous boom set us and the air around us trembling. This was followed by another boom seconds later. I only really understood the situation when I saw the panic in the faces of the others and heard phones begin to ring.

"*Corre!*"—"Run!", my friends shouted. It was a bomb.[37]

I was also afflicted with a serious gastrointestinal disorder and had had enough of "Colombia is passion" (another slogan from an old tourism campaign). In fact, I'd had enough of Colombia full stop. I was ready for New York, for less of the exotic and more of the mainstream.

But what awaited me was something different.

The stuff of dreams
A fateful night on the Playa Blanca

I had just a few days left before I headed off to the Big Apple and because of my health, I wanted to spend them in Bogotá. At the last moment, however, I decided to try to join a Couchsurfing beach camp on the Playa Blanca (White Beach) near Cartagena, hoping for a quick recovery. It was a decision that was to have far-reaching consequences.

The Playa Blanca is one of the white beaches that really earns its name. The fine coral and shell sand caresses your feet, while the warm, turquoise waters beguile your senses. It was there that fate conjured up a magical night of starry skies, fireflies and my first and only experience with crazily luminescent plankton. I fell in love both with that night and the person with whom I shared it, Maria.

We were sitting under a canopy of stars with glow worms in the palm trees behind us, the fine sand under us and the sea before us, when Maria suddenly stood up and led me by the hand into the water.

"*Ven!*"—"Come on!"

We slipped slowly into the sea and the water began to glow with every move we made.

"Have you ever seen anything like it?", I asked Maria.

"No, never ... but it's beautiful", she whispered and pulled me towards her.

And so we floated in an embrace of joy, wonder and love in a fairytale glittering sea.

My very first meeting with Maria a few weeks before had been film-worthy. Habana was a popular bar that offered regular live salsa music and the place was literally cooking every time. Never before and never since have I experienced such a collective ecstasy of dance and music. It's a close call, but it's not even matched by Watergate, near the Oberbaumbrücke in Berlin.

I stepped out into the street for some fresh air only to find this pretty little bundle of fun and before I'd stopped to think about it, I'd asked her to dance. I twirled her around me and suddenly we were in the spotlight of a TV camera and a small group had formed around us. It later emerged that a certain TV star was probably at Habana that night and the TV crew was just there to capture a bit of the vibe before the celebrity interview.

In any case, you could call it a brilliant beginning.

As fate would have it, Maria was studying violin at the music academy and got me a guest performance on a borrowed cello. In an astonishing twist of fate, it emerged that there was a cello professorship open. The director saw me play and the position was suddenly offered to me.

As it turned out, finally getting a work visa took months and included travelling to both Germany and Panama, plenty of bureaucracy and improvisation, and even my first experience with an open request for a bribe, as well as lots of tears and drama.

Eventually, I had all the diplomas and certificates to document, verify and annotate my abilities. I got my visa in Panama. I also got a Colombian identify card for foreign nationals and a bank account. And I got my cello from Germany.

I could finally get started.

I had not dreamt that I would ever teach at a music academy and get to play concerts again, particularly not since I had with a heavy heart and after several final master courses finally closed the door on my cello career several years previously.

And things were to get even better: it turned out that Cartagena was a popular wedding location, particularly among wealthy Americans, which meant there was a constant stream of well-paid gigs. I formed a duo with a violinist who had completed his musical education in Germany and expanded my musical horizons with local musicians in the directions of Latin, jazz and bossa nova.

It was the stuff of dreams.

No-one turns up when it rains

Teaching music in the Caribbean

Unfulfilled dreams definitely have their charm, too, as they remain forever untainted and full of promise. A cello professorship in the Caribbean was in a sense more than anything I could have possibly dreamt of. But as it was a dream come true, I needed a reality check.

While the barriers to entry into the music academy (the Universidad de Bellas Artes Cartagena) had been monumental and required more patience and tenacity than I was aware I possessed, the work that awaited me on a daily basis consisted of even more colossal obstacles, misunderstandings and cultural differences.

It was only after many frantic and frustrated meetings with a brick wall that I learnt to give up. I gave up trying to realise my own ideas in the face of whatever resistance I came up against. I gave up trying to compare what was played there with standards I had previously learnt and trying to fight the mentality of both the students and those responsible for the musical and the administrative direction. I was a guest; I was the cultural other. I despaired that advantage was rarely taken of opportunities to obtain international sponsorship and guest lecturers, that notes and instruments were often missing, and that no-one turned up when it rained. In these situations, I often heard the words *"Profe, tranquilo"*—"Keep your cool, Professor".

Yet, despite this and even though at the beginning of the orchestra rehearsals I was usually sitting almost entirely alone at my desk, with neither instrumentalists nor conductor, I learnt to accept the "miracle" of passable, extremely passionate concerts and to enjoy and celebrate them.

As time went by, I learnt to value every moment of concentrated work with my students and to share the joy of progress with them, to enjoy the pride, satisfaction and happiness on their faces when they completed a student concert or performed well in class. We rarely had a room of our own and some of the students did not possess their own instruments. Others did not even have enough money for the bus. Most of the students had very limited financial resources, something I was able to verify on one or two visits to their slum-like accommodation. As well as being interested in musical and artistic enhancement and progress, these students saw achieving even a modest level of ability as a potential ticket to other programmes in Bogotá or abroad and at the very least to playing music professionally, which for their standards meant substantial amounts of money.

The work was challenging, frustrating and satisfying in equal measure. It was certainly a meaningful occupation.

Waltzing with stage fright
A concert with a cadenza

The successful annual classical music festival in Cartagena is proof that there are few more magical places to celebrate old masterpieces than the colonial squares, imposing churches and courtyards, the huge castle and the renovated old galleon in *el corralito de piedra.*

The fact that the Universidad de Bellas Artes Cartagena itself is in one of the most imposing buildings of the walled centre meant that the history surrounding me always provided a huge inspiration for my musical output. The one the springs to mind is the performance of Shostakovich's *Waltz from the Jazz Suite*:[38]

My heart pounded. That's an understatement. My heart was in my mouth. My hands were sweaty. I was sure to produce a hefty 'natural' vibrato.

The tall, thick stone walls of the old colonial building rose like a kind of nave. At the opposite end of the room were heavy wooden doors with metal fittings. The newly installed air conditioning had worked up until now. At least I didn't have to place a floor fan in front of me like at the Boccherini concert in the cathedral at Easter.

The waltz began with its dialectic of a light, vivacious 3/4 signature and heavy, melancholic main theme. The theme first revealed itself in a shy wind solo. It was then passed on to the violins. Eventually the whole thing built up to a somewhat foolish, shrill and exaggerated climax that somehow still managed to echo, doleful and wistful, somewhere in the hall. Shostakovich is the musical expression of suffering and confusion under Stalin, but perhaps even more significantly, Shostakovich is a deep feeling for beauty and love in defiance of this tragedy.

My fingers steadied themselves in their first position on the fretboard. I went through my solo and the following short cadenza in my head once more. I had 'composed' the latter myself. Preparations were already underway for me; the red carpet was being rolled out. The initial rhythm of the waltz began anew.

I have probably not played enough concerts or solos to experience stage fright as anything less than painful. It stays with some forever. Others say that without it something essential, something almost compulsory, is missing. For me, musical performances have always been something incredibly private—the turning of the deepest inner self to the outside world. With a classical concert there is also the presentation of my most complex and challenging skills, the result of decades of continuous practice with numerous turning points and major doubts.

It truly puts my humble heart to the test. If you then play by heart hundreds (or in the case of pianists many thousands) of notes, fingerings, bow transitions, phrasings, shadings and nuances, emotions are of course particularly volatile. The only thing that helps is to focus on the music and automatisms. Thinking and wanderings of the mind are not really helpful.

And of course, the mind does wander, especially when you are fidgeting around in your chair with nothing yet to do. I brushed the thought aside, took a deep breath and caught the conductor's gaze. My bow arm began to move almost of its own accord.

First, I played the main theme on my cello. This was an arrangement: in the original the trombone comes to the fore at this point. The full, soothing sound of the G string—my favourite string on this cello in particular—gave my mind a little peace.

Then suddenly everything around me was quiet. The music around me dried up in the blink of an eye. The eyes and ears of the entire hall, the orchestra and the conductor were on me. Cadenza.

First a slow variation on the main theme. A few double stops to take it up a notch before the music took off. A vehement increase in pitch and speed, an expressive outburst leading to accelerando arpeggios, only to subside again with the same.

A short while later I merged with the orchestra again via a trill, which seemed to pour out around me. The piece finished with timpani, trumpets and plenty of pomp.

Another image that will forever stay with me is a very early morning in a city that was still empty of people. It was on this day that a new official tourism campaign for Colombia was being filmed. A camera crew from New York had arrived to shoot a short film about the German cellist who had stayed.

The first soft traces of pastel blue were visible in the sky and the old walls were still breathing the nocturnal freshness. A large number of cameras were trained on both myself and on the wind and percussion musicians, who were dressed in the traditional white costumes, typical vueltiao hats and red neckerchiefs. We improvised traditional Colombian rhythms and melodies, and I made an effort to contribute and enter into an exchange with the others.

The layers of sound filled the near-500-year-old square and the range of morning colours constantly expanded until finally, the heat of the day announced its presence.

At home in paradise

An entrepreneur in the Caribbean

Find your inner Latino
Setting up Crazy Salsa

The clapper opened. The clapper closed. The fiery red sphere hung just above the sea, palms fluttered in the wind behind me, and miles of city walls stretched out either side of me. The camera was rolling.

The crew asked me how I'd come to Colombia, why Cartagena of all places and about the story behind our dance school, Crazy Salsa. Although it was still surreal, it was somehow also part of a certain routine that I pragmatically regarded as part of marketing, as part of my work. Colombians are generally proud of their country[39] and are happy when someone shares their enthusiasm and stays there, particularly after the long history of largely negative press the country has received. The story of a German who taught cello and played in the symphony orchestra at the music academy in Cartagena only to then also found a salsa school was welcome and referenced on a regular basis. Local and national television channels and leading print media took up the story: here was another visitor to the country who had discovered that "the only risk is wanting to stay" was more than just a marketing slogan and presented the right marketing message.

So how did Crazy Salsa start? How was it that I actually had a dream job where instead of selling a product, I was conveying lust for life in a picture-postcard Caribbean idyll?

The answer is "with difficulty". The beginning is always hard, and it is particularly hard when you are establishing a company, regardless of where you are. While some processes on Colombia's Caribbean coast might be less formal and consequently sometimes move a little faster or in a less complicated manner ("informal" can often mean the opposite), there were also enough distinct challenges in an emerging tropical market with a long history of political, social and economic instability. In my case, there was also a pretty massive cultural gap. And although being Western European could sometimes be a bonus, it could also quite quickly turn into a disadvantage.

But one step at a time. At first, as is the case with every founder of a company, this required real passion, a certain amount of naive megalomania and the relevant resources.

I had developed and lived out my passion for Afro-Latin American dance after my time in Ghana. These dances continued to represent for me the essence and most direct expression of the very elements of the cultures that I so admired and sought: a combination of flirtatious self-confidence, the ability to devote oneself to the moment and to life without reflection, the joy of and pride in one's own body, and the use of one's body to express positivity and sensuality. Last but not least, it was also dance as a natural, almost inevitable continuation of the spectrum of intense physical communication and social closeness when the mood has reached a certain degree of joy and exuberance.

The posture, the intensity of the facial expressions and the way these people danced (regardless of size or age) gave me the feeling that they were "flirting with life".[40] I saw this as contrasting with the often lifeless posture of most people in Germany, who seem to be literally bent over by the "burden of life".

I saw learning salsa and Afro-Cuban dance as a way for me to find or let loose my inner Latino. The next step (communicating this experience to others and helping them find their inner Latino) is indeed a rewarding task, and during my day-to-day work in Cartagena, I discovered it to be even more rewarding than I had ever imagined. Many tourists regarded what they had learnt and experienced during our lessons and with our teachers as the best thing they took home with them. What I loved about the job was being able to fill a few hours of people's precious holiday time with fun and provide them with new skills for the rest of their lives. In several cases, these experiences also led to very intense personal moments and lasting friendships.

What more can you hope to achieve with your work?

Another aspect with regard to passion that should not be underestimated was the fact that the Caribbean dream I was living at the time would have soon ended had I not found additional sources of income to my job as cello professor. It was several months before the start of the semester at the music academy and even longer before I actually received my first salary payment. As I would later discover in my work with start-ups in Germany, a certain amount of financial pressure (or even a complete absence of finances) really plays a role in generating the intensity and resilient doggedness with which people who start companies pursue their ideas through the inevitable setbacks and stalemates.

Don't forget that my relentless need to get things done also drove me on. Stretching a comparison, you might regard my trip around the world as a full-time job in the sense it was a never-ending flood of events, of planning, packing, trying to find a couch and being on the road. This abated with all the rigmarole involved in obtaining visas or waiting for some authority or authorisation or other. In the initial phase of founding the school, I regarded whatever stood in my way as a welcome sparring partner.

Was it a naive delusion of grandeur? Or perhaps just being ballsy?[41] A certain amount of balls was what was needed in this situation. Many people (especially Colombians) laughed at the idea in the beginning. In other countries (probably the best example being Cuba), the potential of dance holidays and dance courses as an essential part of the holiday experience has been identified and put into practice. In Cartagena, however, there was no other dedicated dance school for tourists when I founded Crazy Salsa. But that wasn't all. At first, none of the discussions with the tour operators or tourism agencies came to anything, because, like most other Cartageneros, they didn't understand why someone should or would spend money on learning something that everyone can do "naturally". They saw even less potential to make decent money with it.

This brings us to resources. Since my savings were very modest, my first approach was to cooperate with local dance clubs. It took several weeks of bitter setbacks and disappointments before I learnt to separate superficial enthusiasm and consent from serious interest in a business partnership and then to secure such a partnership.

The only initial investments were the shared costs for a mirror wall, as well as a few flyers, posters and t-shirts, a banner and a website. The investment for the website was limited to production and hosting costs, since I did the content, design and programming myself. My further education course in web design had paid off after all.

Then it was time to go out, put up posters in hotels and hostels, hand out flyers and learn how to use doormen as a distribution channel. The latter attempt turned out to be a rather tricky and ultimately not entirely cost-free venture.

We started with a few hours on selected days and early evenings. The deal was that the bar would earn from the drinks and additional audience, and would also receive a certain percentage of the revenue. Our bestseller was a crash course entitled "Get Ready for the Cartagena Nights", which included the most important Latin moves and the basics of the most popular dances. It also wasn't long before we found customers for private lessons. There were of course some evenings on which we spent the whole time sitting around only for no-one to show up, which wasn't a great feeling.

On other days, however, a real group dynamic developed for our crash courses in the hostels and we had a full house. The growing volume of private lessons filled the coffers; we soon paid off our initial outlay and were in the black.

We had reached an important milestone. It was a moment to savour.

Not a bad life
Auditioning dance instructors

The streets were still largely quiet. It was too early for fruit sellers, students or hordes of tourists.

After opening the iron latch and several locks (yet another had been added since the break-in) on the metal grill, I opened the grill doors outwards and pulled the old wooden doors behind them inwards to let the light spill into the room. The sun was relentless even in the morning.

I stuck the posters with the schedule and prices on the side of the door facing the street and opened the windows in both *salas*. A brief click and the ceiling fan in the front room began its languid, slightly wobbly rotations before—to my great relief—purring and whirring into life.

A brief examination of the wall provided another source of relief: the termites had neither reoccupied nor begun to reconstruct their old channels. My gaze turned to the large mirrors and to the murals of colonial city walls and romantic dance scenes.

The stylised figures in the colourful nocturnal parade invited onlookers to dance. I smiled, as I almost always did when I looked at the image. We had been blessed by the simple fact that the painter, a friend of mine, had produced a masterpiece. I loved the slightly provocative facial expressions and poses. They weren't too extreme to be salacious, but they were enough to convey to the observer a certain amount of cheek and naive merriment. I couldn't get enough of the colours of the clothes and I was repeatedly wowed by the embellishments that ran around the entire wall, depicting the city's core colours in pastel hues: the pale blue of the ocean, the earthy ochre of the sand, the soft grey-brown tones of the city walls, the fresh green of the palms and the gentle, reddish-yellow wash of the sun.

I quickly checked the state of the toilets. Although the ceiling was still damp and warped, the improvements that had been made since the last tropical rains appeared to have held. Another click to start the air-conditioning in the main room. I waited a moment to check whether it really was getting cooler. Again, I was grateful to discover nothing that could cause any fear of another incident.

I started the computer, connected it to the credit card machine, slipped out of my sandals and ran my feet over the cool floor. How I enjoyed spending every day of the year in light summer clothing and sandals without a single pullover in my cupboard.

I quickly looked through the new customer enquiries and the agencies' notifications of bookings, checked that the various websites were in sync and then turned to the list of the dancers invited that day. I prepared my questions and went over to the stereo to find a few suitable tunes.

A little later the first candidate was standing in the doorway, a broad smile on her face. We kissed our greetings and got going.

"*A bailar!*"—"Let's dance!"

While a friendly, up-beat attitude, a basic command of English (depending on the scenario) and an ability to dance (obviously) were important, the most crucial thing was the ability and willingness to accept a certain amount of method in the approach to instruction.

As we taught salsa, merengue and bachata, as well as Afro-Colombian and local dances (later we even offered dance aerobics—primarily for locals), we provided a broad spectrum of dances and had a lot of dance instructors on our books. Most of our day-to-day business was entrusted to a small group of established instructors, who had proved themselves to be trustworthy and to whom we quickly felt a close bond.

Auditioning the dance instructors was without doubt one of my highlights as owner of the dance school. Those who do the teaching are, after all, the heart and soul of such a business and if you feel personally responsible for the quality of the lessons and customer satisfaction, finding and keeping suitable instructors is the most important task.

When this most important task involves creating, designing and putting up posters to recruit instructors, a nice chat with young dancers and a few practice dances, then life is going pretty well.

Dancing for joy

Stories from the dance school

How did we teach people to find their inner Latino? Who taught? More importantly, what did they teach and how?

It helped that I had danced, assisted and co-hosted some dances at a salsa school in Berlin and had performed with the Afro-Cuban show group. It also helped that I had got to know a good concept for such a dance school in Cuba, as well as the promising one-on-one approach, according to which each student has a local dance partner. This provides an intense and immediate experience from the outset. It also creates a bond that provides a reasonable (if not an absolute) guarantee that the student will return.

In accordance with the primary goal of using the dances as a medium for conveying the Latin American way of life, the key points of focus were isolation exercises, developing a feel for the music and the various rhythms, and internalising the basic steps. Turns and figures were always of secondary importance; they were more ornamental than a central component—a playful extra. The goal was to get the students to move freely to the music within just a few hours and for them to enjoy their interaction with the rhythms and close communication with their partners.

In Cartagena in particular, several dance partners were almost outraged by an excess of turns.

"No soy una muñequita!"— "I'm not a puppet!", they would say. *"Con sabor!"*

What they wanted was to feel the music in their partner's body; they wanted *sabor* (taste). They did not want to perform a dance show. In most other parts of the world in which I have travelled (from North

America and Europe to Asia and Australia) salsa is more about show, technique and competition, at least it is when the Latino contingent is relatively small. Luckily, there is no arguing about taste, and there is no question that both interpretations and styles are justified. In Colombia alone you can find almost every conceivable variation, and Cali in particular is famous for its shows.

In the beginning, Maria and I taught and recruited other dance partners from our circle of friends for larger classes. But soon we had well-trained instructors who were able to teach the students the Crazy Salsa method, as well as a feel for the dance and the attitude to life, with real authenticity and a personal touch.

Some of the most satisfying experiences of this time included little cinematic stories of a particularly heart-rending kind. As you can well imagine, dancing is an essential part of social life and especially of celebrating in Colombia. For many, a party without dancing simply isn't a party. If Cupid fires an arrow and causes an American man to fall in love with a Colombian woman, the American may find he is missing an essential ability—one that is required to fully participate in social life and particularly in life's most beautiful and joyous moments (including but not limited to weddings and the like). There were several instances in which we provided very intensive "secret" lessons for a rather awkward mover so that he could then, at a special moment, surprise his beloved by taking her hand and leading her onto the dance floor, skilfully placing her at the centre of attention with a natural hip-rolling, ass-shaking nonchalance that even included the mandatory complacent, almost bored pathos.

The most touching story that we experienced, however, involved a somewhat older, well-to-do Colombian from the highlands. Although he would probably never have dared lower his guard in front of a fellow countryman, he accepted my "authority" and spent long hours of practice so that he could proudly ask his daughter for the first dance at her wedding.

One becomes two
The business begins to grow

From a business perspective, a dance school for tourists is rather limited in terms of potential for growth. It was only in exceptional cases that tourists came to Cartagena specifically for a few hours of dance lessons a day. Going to the dance school was usually only one of the activities they had booked there. We achieved some growth through cooperation and appropriate online marketing. We were also able to expand the product range and to upsell by offering traditional dance costumes, explanations of how they are made and visits to tailors, dance shows, choreography for surprise dances at weddings, merchandise and a few other things, including even monthly dance aerobics and hosting our own dance parties.[42]

However, it was also clear from my previous personal experience of the customer's point of view that the real potential lay in combining dance classes with language holidays. People learning Spanish tend to stay for three or four, sometimes as many as eight, weeks and take not one or two, but four to six hours of lessons a day. The classes are also usually larger and the students have plenty of time for dancing and other activities during the rest of the day.

It didn't take a business genius to see that there was a wealth of riches waiting there. However, without substantial funds of our own to invest, we first went the route of cooperating with existing Spanish schools and having our dance classes included in the packages for language students. Since willingness was very thin, we were more or less pushed into opening our own language school. The moment came when the salsa school slowly grew and we rented a studio with two rooms. Since we now had (and had paid for) the premises for the whole day anyway and since the dance classes were usually held in the late afternoon, it was only really a small step to have tables and boards made for us, to buy chairs and teaching materials, and to hire the first teachers. One had become two.

The global language course market is extremely competitive: in principle, a school in Cartagena is competing with schools throughout the Spanish-speaking world. Suddenly the combination with the salsa school was one of the Spanish school's biggest assets. We also developed a host family model for which we personally selected certain families and offered the option of integrating the students into family life if they so desired. The packages that included diving courses and the opportunity to take parts of the course on the beach under palm trees proved very successful.

The breakthrough, however, came from an unexpected source. Unlike the market for dance lessons, the market for Spanish lessons is not usually an end-customer market from the point of view of the respective school. What happens in reality is that specialised language travel providers (mainly from Western countries) act as intermediaries between the end-customer and schools offering various languages in various countries.

One enquiry from a European language travel agency later we had concluded an agreement that provided the starting point for much greater utilisation of the school's capacity and more international contracts.

Suddenly, we had a constant stream of student groups and the revenue per customer increased drastically, as most of them booked several weeks of both dance and language courses with accommodation. It wasn't long before the language school even became an accredited provider of paid educational leave for German citizens.

Our baby was growing up.

Life under the palm trees
Just another day in paradise

As Cartagena lies just above the equator, the sun rises at almost exactly six in the morning and sets at six in the evening throughout the year. The temperatures are nearly constant at 30–32° C during the day and 25–27° C at night—365 days a year. The first few months of the year are usually dry and there is a delightfully refreshing wind. In the latter months of the year there are thunderstorms almost every day, you sweat almost constantly, and even the locals shower and change their clothes several times a day if they can.

My days often began before daybreak. As I was usually giving dance lessons or performing music in the evenings, this was the only opportunity to go jogging out of the searing glare of the sun. Running has been a fundamental part of my life since I was a boy and is essential for my physical well-being and for gathering my thoughts, so I needed all my willpower to drag myself out of bed by five at the latest. The joy of running in the morning was that I could jog along the seafront almost undisturbed, watching the fiery orb rise over the old city walls and then, after a refreshing shower, start the day revitalised. An evening swim was my alternative for a proper physical workout. This was made possible by a Swiss friend of mine who lived in a modern apartment complex in the north of the city. It had a large swimming pool with a view of the sea. If time allowed, I might also go for an early morning run along the colonial city wall as the sun dipped into the sea and couples began to build their love nests in the wall's many little recesses.

Waking up in a tropical climate is easy. Your body is warm and you're ready to start the day as soon as your eyes are open. I'd let the ceiling fan run all night and the heat would be back in the room as soon as I turned it off. The first shower of the day was always pleasantly rejuvenating. There was no way to regulate the shower temperature. The water simply came out as it was in the pipe, which at the outside temperatures was more often warm than cold.

I'd throw on a pair of shorts and a T-shirt, or, alternatively, the typical white linen clothes of Cartagena, which were ideal for the climate. The shirt is often embroidered, which lends a certain elegance to this otherwise simple traditional dress.

Then I'd slip into a pair of leather Colombian flip-flops, sling my cello over my shoulder and go out into the street to flag down one of the shared taxis.

As the taxis were usually extremely small (a Chevrolet Spark or something of a similar size) and three usually sat in the back, it was cramped and hot. But I still loved the ten-minute ride along the beach into the historic city centre, the sea air and a feeling of being on holiday despite the fact I was on my way to work. I never really regarded what I did as work (at least in the sense of a "normal" job in Germany), even though I was busy seven days a week and quite often from eight in the morning to ten or eleven at night. It was my life and at that point in time it was the life I wanted. The cello classes, orchestra practices, salsa lessons, interviews, answering customers' questions on the computer and creating the website were as much part of my day as hanging out at one of the Old Town's squares or on the city walls with friends, taking a boat to one of the neighbouring islands or long nights of dancing.

Breakfast was usually a couple of bananas, a packet of delicious salted green mango sticks from one of the market women, or one or two empanadas (little baked or fried pastries filled with cheese, chicken or beef). After a cool coconut, a fresh passionfruit juice or a guava juice (my favourite), I was ready to take on any challenge.

The music academy is a prestigious colonial-style building with red panelling on the outside and white panelling on the inside. It is located in the centre of the picturesque Old Town, which is home to colourful houses, flower-festooned balconies, a multitude of churches and the spectacular landmark of the cathedral. The university's central courtyard is lined with shady porticoes and one of the historic centre's many squares unfolds before the mighty iron-clad wooden gate at the entrance. Not far behind it is the city wall and behind that the Caribbean Sea stretches to the horizon. Waves gently lap against the promenade.

My work typically began in one of the classrooms behind one of the porticoes. As there was no air-conditioning and there were only open wooden windows, it was sweaty and working on music was made difficult by the sound of music coming in from every angle and students practising in the corridors. For this to happen, of course, the students first needed to actually be there, which was not always the case. I often had to wait a long time or the students didn't come at all, which often gave me plenty of time to practise for my performances and concerts.

I almost always went home for lunch, as Maria's family's domestic helper always prepared a delicious meal. Domestic helpers are very common among the middle classes. I learnt that they often earn no more than 100 Euros a month, that they work most of the day and that they take on all of the housework—from washing and cleaning to cooking. There was usually a lentil or bean stew and a plate with a small piece of meat, rice or fried plantain and a salad with fresh limes.

Before I returned to the centre, there would be a few minutes for my second shower and a quick snooze directly on the comparatively cool stone floor under one of the ceiling fans.

In the afternoon there were more classes and an orchestra rehearsal. In both the mornings and afternoons, both Maria and I would often head over to our language and dance school to attend to various matters. We had been able to rent a space for our school just three minutes' walk from the music academy. Spanish classes were usually from nine in the morning to midday and from one to four in the afternoon, while the salsa classes began at five in the evening and ended between eight and ten. While our work for the Spanish classes was limited to administrative tasks and our main job was to ensure that all the students were satisfied, we usually took an active role in the dance lessons (particularly in the first year) and there was always plenty to do in advising prospective customers and planning the details of the classes.

As soon as the last classes were finished, we would head to one of the squares or the city walls to see out the day with a few friends, Couchsurfers, customers or students with a few soft drinks or beers. Dinner typically consisted of arepas (maize flatbread with a rich filling of vegetables and meat) or the local versions of the hamburger.

If musicians had gigged that night and had a little extra cash in their pockets, they'd shout several more rounds after the first drink. The way they looked at life was clearly focused on the moment and enjoying and sharing it with friends rather than saving the takings from such gigs. On wild evenings, beer was followed by aguardiente, a Colombian aniseed schnapps: everyone would be given a small plastic cup and drank a round.

And if the dance students still wanted to party with us, we'd began a long night in Cartagena's numerous dance clubs. Another advantage of having the warm sea on our doorstep was being able to peel off our clothes and end a fantastic night out by jumping into the water. Sleep would then overtake me within seconds of the ceiling fan whirring into life.

Farewell to summer, sun and sandals

The limits of paradise

With a professorship, the symphony orchestra, solo concerts, gigs and dance lessons, as well as responsibility for administration, sales, marketing, HR and operations for two businesses, I was never bored. It was 24/7, but I loved pretty much every minute of it and really poured my heart into it.

There were also some hefty low blows, which included burglary, water damage, termite infestation, misappropriation of income by teachers and a suspicion of an imminent protection racket.

Family members in Germany became seriously ill, several close friends and family members married, my first nephews and nieces were born and the question of a long-term life plan slowly began to dawn.

I was practically on the beach. Non-stop summer, sun and sandals. I was in love and engaged. My time in Cartagena was of course something that I could never have dreamt of. I lived in what was without doubt a beautiful place with great weather and a lively social life. I had suddenly become an entrepreneur and professor. I had succeeded in putting two of my great passions, music and dance, at the centre of my professional life. With the salsa school, I had succeeded in making the conveyance of my lust for life the core of my professional life. I was regularly in front of the camera or doing interviews. I lived in a culture that I admired so much in many respects and in which, in many ways, I felt more at home than in Germany.

And yet I did not belong here and never would. No matter how well I could speak Spanish, no matter how well I might dance, no matter how well I might assimilate myself in terms of traditional costume and skin tone.

And it was not a place I could imagine starting a family. My assessment of risks took a different perspective. Professional and financial stability took on a different face and weight; they had gradually become what I longed for rather than what I was rebelling against. I no longer wanted 1000 cool friends all over the world; I wanted two close friends nearby.

It was time to go home.

The joys of life and bundles of joy

Home sweet home

A great tectonic plate shift had begun within me, without me being immediately aware of it. A mismatch between my self-model and my changing geography slowly emerged.

One of the first consequences was the rather painful end of what had been in many respects (especially when viewed from the outside) a fairytale relationship. It also meant cutting ties with the dance and language schools in the medium term, as this involvement still intertwined my life with that of my ex-fiancé. However, the two companies continued to thrive: both recently celebrated their tenth anniversaries (Crazy Salsa in 2018 and BABEL International Language Institute in 2019).

Although it took me a little time and understanding before I fully realised it, my top priority was to start a family and have children. Globetrotting and the search for a vocation in the sense of a professional occupation were no longer the decisive and primary determinant for planning my life.

I came to understand that this also involved a considerable increase in the importance of building a nest and a life that allowed for greater resilience and stability.

I am still mulling over the extent of the developments I have briefly described here today. It was and still is the result of the fact that it had become necessary to make permanent, long-term connections and compromises in terms of partners and friends, and also in terms of work, place of residence and culture. It was not only necessary to simply make connections, but also to learn to love this life.

I started this new journey with a heart full of adventures, sensations, countries and people. I was still inspired by seemingly limitless freedom and the "fame" of my stories.

However, I had neither a spoon nor a cent to my name, no local circle of friends and no career in the Western sense. I also had a new partner, who had given up her life in Russia for our common dream and at first did not speak a word of German. She also had no job and no money. And I still had my high demands and ambitions. In the provincial, small-town atmosphere of Heidelberg, surrounded by so many people with a house, career and family, I felt more of a stranger and had even less sense of belonging than perhaps ever before.

An enormous mountain range suddenly rose up before me. The only road ahead was a stony path that led along many an abyss and through many an icy storm.

Once I was finally married, once my wife and I had found stable jobs and a comfortably furnished apartment, once I felt at home in Heidelberg and once I had a wide circle of friends, I'd gone a little greyer.

The birth of my first daughter two years ago is probably the greatest miracle and joy that life has brought me so far. It was also the beginning of another completely new journey.

It was a journey with more belonging and love than at any previous point in my life. And it was a new type of freedom: freedom from options, freedom from the challenge of reinventing myself and reshaping my life every day. My daughter now defined my tasks and role and I experienced this (for the most part) as liberating.

Hearing "Papa!" or catching a glance from my daughter is enough for me to condense the entire universe into the moment, to be present in my entire being and with every fibre of my body.

Playing with my daughter, seeing and sensing how much she trusts me, how happy she is to see me and how much she loves me, is the epitome of meaning in my life; it is my ultimate calling. There is nothing I would rather do and there is no place on Earth I would rather be.

Freedom and belonging

Epilogue

When you have a bindle and fiddle or a knapsack on your back, a light breeze in your face and the world at your feet, the freedom of solo travel is a real rush.

The flow of travelling, complete absorption in the moment, the constant stream of new impressions and experiences, images and smells, people and flavours is enchanting.

In many ways, solo travel—like the hospitality you experience—brings out the best in people:[43] trust, generosity, solidarity, tolerance, love and connection with people and nature irrespective of any borders.

Travelling in rural areas and meeting people who still have limited contact with modern mass society and consumer society is for many—including myself—a real revelation.

As a traveller, you also become a child again somewhere along the way. You observe, marvel, imitate and regularly gain a new awareness of the limitations of both the way you see the world and the way you see yourself.

Travel is also an interplay between solitude and belonging that gives rise to a deep closeness to oneself. What is it that emerges as both the constant in all these contrasting experiences and the unifying factor for the reflections of oneself in the foreign? It is nothing less than an encounter with one's multifaceted self (many aspects of which have been newly discovered), which ultimately leads to a new, deeper, richer perception of oneself.

Freedom is liberating in the sense of being free from restrictive rules, constraints and limitations. But freedom is also being unconnected, uprooted, alone.

Those who are free in the truest sense of the word have no ties whatsoever. This is something I have lived out to the extreme. The experience can be exciting and for a while appropriate in a phase of youthful exuberance, adventure and discovery. However, resilient relationships, connections and even identification with places, people and topics require bonds. And with it there is also give and take. There are compromises. There are restrictions on personal freedom.

The promise of the modern consumer society is different: you alone are master of your destiny, you do not need anyone, any responsibility is yours alone, you have the choice. If it is too cold where you are, move to a warmer place; if your partner is not suitable, find another; if you are not in a good mood, consume this or get a prescription for that. If you then identify yourself primarily through your consumer behaviour, be it food, sport, clothing, cars, travel or even your choice of job or partner, you escape the need for reciprocity and connection by exchanging them for an even greater dependence on these consumed endowers of meaning and identity.

Freedom is the availability of options[44] and therefore always also means responsibility. The freedom lies in the choice to decide into which bonds and dependencies you wish to enter. The goal of freedom as permanent detachment from dependencies and compromises is a mirage and results in a state of permanent loneliness.

But the freedom of the traveller can also be coupled with or alternate with a deep feeling of connectedness.

In other countries (especially in Ghana, where I had my first formative experience of extended solo travelling), I was often touched by the intensity of human closeness and warmth. And although or precisely because I was just an observer, a stranger, this generated a warm feeling of connectedness with all people and with the human experience.

I felt a primeval, prehistoric connection in the red dust of Australia's Outback and was intoxicated by the feeling of being part of and losing myself in this fascinating world while diving into the underwater kingdoms of the Great Barrier Reef.

Vipassana has allowed me to experience unity and connectedness with myself, my life and above all with all people, with life in its entirety, even with the eternal laws of the universe.

The often intense and intimate relationships with the people I met while travelling (most whom I met through Couchsurfing and hospitality) have made the world a single family. This was perhaps nowhere more explicit than during the time I spent in the "commune" of international harvest workers in Riverland.

Whether you find happiness in feeling settled and a sense of belonging at home or in a feeling of being connected with the entire world on your travels, is it not the image of love as the awareness of being connected—to another person, a community, nature, the universe, God, home or oneself—that unites the two and is what every human being is searching for?

Endnotes and links

¹ St. Aubin de Terán, Lisa (1996). Off the Rails. London: Sceptre.

² Lee, Laurie (1969). As I Walked Out One Midsummer Morning. London: Penguin.

³ Although this is usually attributed to John Lennon in his lyrics to "Beautiful Boy (Darling Boy)", the expression probably goes back to the writer Allen Saunders (https://en.wikipedia.org/wiki/Allen_Saunders, accessed 24/05/2018).

⁴ Also known as the Fula or Fulɓe people.

⁵ Incredible India is the name of an Indian tourism agency and campaign that has run since 2002.

⁶ http://www.taz.de/!5473491/, accessed 07/01/ 2018.

⁷ Osho (2013). Living On Your Own Terms. New York: St. Martin's Griffin.

⁸ Couchsurfing included many, many more cities, not only Western metropolises. This selection only serves as personal example, as I travelled to these cities and was able to experience some of the local communities myself.

⁹ I find a particularly beautiful version of this hospitality for God in the story *Where Love Is, God Is* by Leo Tolstoy (1885).

¹⁰ Jaucourt, Louis, chevalier de, The Encyclopedia of Diderot & d'Alembert Collaborative Translation Project. Translated by Sophie Bourgault. Ann Arbor: Michigan Publishing, University of Michigan Library, 2013. Web, accessed 29/05/2020. http://hdl.handle.net/2027/spo.did2222.0002.761. Trans. of "Hospitalité", "Encyclopédie ou Dictionnaire

raisonné des sciences, des arts et des métiers", Vol. 8. Paris, 1765.

[11] Hirschfeld, Christian (1777). Von der Gastfreundschaft: Eine Apologie für die Menschheit. Leipzig: Weidmann und Reich.

[12] L.L. Zamenhof, in a letter to Nikolai Borovko, approx. 1895.

[13] From the poem "La Espero" by Zamenhof.

[14] Luitweiler, Bob (1999). The Seeds of Servas: Opening Doors for Peace. San Francisco: Richard Piro.

[15] see Luitweiler, Bob (1999).

[16] Broadbridge, Edward; Jonas, Uffe; Warren, Clay (2011). The School for Life: N.F.S. Grundtvig on Education for the People. Aarhus: Aarhus University Press.

[17] Highlander Research and Education Center, previously known as Highlander Folk School, Tennessee. https://highlandercenter.org, accessed 19/04/2022.

[18] see Luitweiler, Bob (1999).

[19] see Luitweiler, Bob (1999).

[20] J. William Fulbright, initiator of the Fulbright Scholarship Program offered an apt quote on this subject in an address he made to the Council on International Educational Exchange in 1983: "Educational exchange can turn nations into people, contributing as no other form of communication can to the humanizing of international relations." https://eca.state.gov/fulbright/about-fulbright, accessed 24/05/2018.

[21] As well as Couchsurfing, I used other social networks on my travels to meet people there and get a taste of everyday life. Meetup.com was the next most important platform after Couchsurfing.

[22] World Wide Opportunities on Organic Farms.

[23] see Lee, Laurie (1969).

[24] https://www.welt.de/gesundheit/article2145584/Dick-dicker-und-Australier.html, accessed 25/06/2008.

[25] https://theconversation.com/urban-sprawl-is-threatening-sydneys-foodbowl-55156, accessed 24/02/2016,

[26] StudiVZ was an online community of similar popularity to Facebook on the German-speaking market at the time.

[27] There are now additional working holiday agreements with countries such as South Korea, Taiwan and Hong Kong.

[28] The version presented here is as taught by S.N. Goenka.

[29] Hart, William (1987). The Art of Living: Vipassana Meditation as taught by S.N. Goenka. New York: Harper Collins.

[30] "What We Do Together: The State of Associational Life in America", May 2017, study as part of the "Social Capital Project" in Utah, commissioned by Senator Mike Lee. https://www.jec.senate.gov/public/index.cfm/republicans/2017/5/what-we-do-together-the-state-of-associational-life-in-america, accessed 28/02/2022.

[31] Kendrick, D.T., Vladas, G., Neuberg, S.L., & Schaller, M. (2010). "Renovating the pyramid of needs: Contemporary extensions built upon ancient foundations", Perspectives in Psychological Sciences, 5(3), 292-314. doi: 10.1177/1745691610369469.

[32] Study of Adult Development at Harvard University, TED Talk https://www.ted.com/talks/robert_waldinger_what_m

akes_a_good_life_lessons_from_the_longest_study_ on_happiness, accessed 26/05/2018.

[33] see Study of Adult Development at Harvard University, TED Talk (2018)

[34] Diamond, Jared (2012). The World Until Yesterday. London: Penguin.

[35] Wulf, A. (2015). The Invention of Nature: Alexander von Humboldt's New World. New York: Knopf.

[36] Krengel, Martin (2015). Stoppt die Welt – Ich will aussteigen! – Kuriose Abenteuer einer Weltreise. (Arschtritt inklusive). Berlin: Eazybookz Travel.

[37] As I was there before the final peace treaty, the bombs were probably part of a FARC protection racket. No people were harmed in this case.

[38] The piece described is usually known as *Waltz from the Jazz Suite*. However, it has been discovered that the waltz comes from the *Suite for Variety Orchestra* and is not part of the *Suite for Jazz Orchestra No. 2*.

[39] This generalisation is used to describe a significant, dominant and unique aspect of the culture. There are of course, as always, exceptions to the rule.

[40] This is the origin of the title of this book. The phrase struck me as a description of the lightness, provocative pride, and joyful abandon of the gait, especially in the way people danced in my temporarily adopted home in the Caribbean. The people sometimes seemed to be "flirting with life" a little bit in their every step, every movement, every look. I found the quote by Lisa Saint Aubin de Terán later, while checking to see if the title had been used before.

[41] The Spanish term is *"cojones"* or *"huevos"* and is used with both great frequency and gusto.

[42] Our own events, live music, a bar and a permit to serve alcohol followed much later, when I was no longer involved in the business.

[43] Of course, travelling as experiencing the world and yourself is different from travelling as relaxation or simply sightseeing and ticking off items on a bucket list. These are simply two quite different things that are often thrown together under the same name.

[44] Sen, Amartya (2005). Development as Freedom. New York: Oxford University Press.

Further reading

Books that inspire travelling

Dunn, Ross E. (2012). The Adventures of Ibn Battuta: A Muslim Traveller of the Fourteenth Century. Berkeley: University of California Press.

Hirschfeld, Christian (1777). Von der Gastfreundschaft: Eine Apologie für die Menschheit. Leipzig: Weidmann und Reich.

Kapuściński, Ryszard (2016). The Shadow of the Sun. New York: Knopf.

Kieran, Dan (2012). The Idle Traveller: The Art of Slow Travel. Basingstoke: Automobile Association.

Klaus, Johannes (2016). The Travel Episodes – Neue Geschichten für Abenteurer, Glücksritter und Tagträumer. Berlin: Piper.

Klaus, Johannes (2016). The Travel Episodes – Geschichten von Fernweh und Freiheit. Berlin: Piper.

Körner, Fabius Sixtus (2013). Journey Man – 1 Mann, 5 Kontinente und jede Menge Jobs. Berlin: Ullstein.

Krengel, Martin (2015). Stoppt die Welt – Ich will aussteigen! – Kuriose Abenteuer einer Weltreise. (Arschtritt inklusive). Berlin: Eazybookz Travel.

Lee, Laurie (1969). As I Walked Out One Midsummer Morning. London: Penguin.

Luitweiler, Bob (1999). The Seeds of Servas: Opening Doors for Peace. San Francisco: Richard Piro.

Sieböck, Gregor (2011). Der Weltenwanderer – Zu Fuß um die halbe Welt. Munich: Piper.

Stewart, Chris (1999). Driving over Lemons: An Optimist in Andalucia. London: Sort Of Books.

Timmerberg, Helge (2004). Tiger fressen keine Yogis. Berlin: Piper.

Trojanow, Ilija (2009). The Collector of Worlds. London: Faber & Faber.

Recommended reading on evolution, religion and culture

Boyer, P. (2001). Religion Explained: The Evolutionary Origins of Religious Thought. New York: Basic Books.

Broadbridge, Edward; Jonas, Uffe; Warren, Clay (2011). The School for Life: N.F.S. Grundtvig on Education for the People. Aarhus: Aarhus University Press.

Carson, Clayborne (1998). The Autobiography of Martin Luther King, Jr. London: Abacus.

Diamond, Jared (2005). Guns, Germs, and Steel: The Fates of Human Societies. New York: Norton.

Diamond, Jared (2012). The World Until Yesterday. London: Penguin.

Ganten, Detlev; Deichmann, Thomas; Spahl, Thilo (2009). Die Steinzeit steckt uns in den Knochen. Gesundheit als Erbe der Evolution. Munich: Piper-Verlag.

Graziano, Michael S. A. (2013). Consciousness and the Social Brain. Oxford: Oxford University Press.

Harari, Yuval Noah (2014). Sapiens: A Brief History of Humankind. London: Harvill Secker.

Harari, Yuval Noah (2016). Homo Deus: A Brief History of Tomorrow. London: Harvill Secker.

Hobsbawm, Eric (1968). Industry and Empire: The Birth of the Industrial Revolution. London: Penguin.

Hofstede, G., & Hofstede, G.J. (2005). Cultures and Organizations: Software of the Mind. New York: McGraw-Hill.

Obama, Barack (2004). Dreams from My Father: A Story of Race and Inheritance. New York: Three Rivers Press.

Sass, Stephen L. (1998). The Substance of Civilization: Materials and Human History form the Stone Age to the Age of Silicon. New York: Arcade.

Sen, Amartya (1999). Development as Freedom. Oxford: Oxford University Press.

Wulf, A. (2015). The Invention of Nature: Alexander von Humboldt's New World. New York: Knopf.

Further reading on community and cooperation

Block, Peter (2009), Community: The Structure of Belonging. Oakland: Berrett-Kohler.

Nowak, Martin A.; Highfield, Roger (2011). Super Cooperators: Altruism, Evolution, and Why We Need Each Other to Succeed. New York: Free Press.

Putnam, Robert D. (2000). Bowling Alone: The Collapse and Revival of American Community. New York: Simon & Schuster.

Vogel, Charles H. (2016): The Art of Community: Seven Principles for Belonging. Oakland: Berrett-Kohler.

Printed in Great Britain
by Amazon